'Men who are Determined to be Free'

The American Assault on Stony Point, 15 July 1779

David C. Bonk

Helion & Company Limited
Unit 8 Amherst Business Centre
Budbrooke Road
Warwick
CV34 5WE
England
Tel. 01926 499 619
Fax 0121 711 4075
Email: info@helion.co.uk
Website: www.helion.co.uk
Twitter: @helionbooks
Visit our blog at http://blog.helion.co.uk/

Published by Helion & Company 2018
Designed and typeset by Farr Out Publications, Wokingham, Berkshire
Cover designed by Paul Hewitt, Battlefield Design (www.battlefield-design.co.uk)
Printed by Henry Ling Limited, Dorchester, Dorset

Text © David C. Bonk 2018
Original artwork by Ed Dovey, © Helion & Company 2018; other images as credited
Maps drawn by George Anderson © Helion & Company 2018

Cover: 'The Assault on the Upper Works at Stony Point' by Ed Dovey, © Helion & Company 2018

ISBN 978-1-912174-84-3

British Library Cataloguing-in-Publication Data.
A catalogue record for this book is available from the British Library.

For details of other military history titles published by Helion & Company Limited, contact the above
address, or visit our website: http://www.helion.co.uk

We always welcome receiving book proposals from prospective authors.

Contents

Introduction

The Hudson Highlands loom large in the history of the American Revolution. Both American commander George Washington and British commander Sir Henry Clinton recognized early in the struggle that the Hudson River and the surrounding hills and valleys represented a natural barrier to movement between New England and the Middle Colonies. The rugged landscape and limited crossings of the Hudson River made campaigning in the region challenging. For the Americans, control of the Hudson River crossings would ensure the uninterrupted flow of men and supplies from New England into the seat of war in Pennsylvania, New York and New Jersey. For the British, isolating the New England colonies from the rest of the lower colonies would have significant strategic benefits, denying the Continental Army critical resources. In addition, control of the Hudson Highlands would expedite communication with British forces in Canada and threaten the strategic center of Albany.

The clash at Stony Point in 1779 was the last episode in struggle for supremacy in the Hudson Highlands, and its capture by Wayne's light infantry represented a signal victory for Washington and the Continental cause in a year characterized by frustrating maneuvering for strategic advantage by both sides.

The assault on Stony Point reflected the personalities and experiences of the principle antagonists: Sir Henry Clinton; George Washington; and Brigadier General Anthony Wayne. Clinton returned to the Hudson Highlands in May 1779 out of a state of exasperation with the overall stalemate which had characterized the war since the British had evacuated Philadelphia in June 1778. Despite assurances given by the British government that he would have freedom of action upon replacing Sir William Howe as Commander-in-Chief of the British armies in American in June 1778, Clinton continued to be burdened with interference by Lord George Germain, Secretary of State for America, and others in the British government. Attempting to manage a war over 3,500 miles of ocean through directives written three to four months earlier was an open invitation for misunderstandings and missed opportunities. Promised British reinforcements, intended to support these strategic directives, were either delayed or redirected to other theaters at the same time as portions of Clinton's command were ordered away from New York. Faced with dwindling resources and orders to shift the locus of the war to the southern Colonies, Clinton was anxious to bring Washington and the Continental Army into a decisive showdown.

Understanding the importance of the Hudson Highlands to the American cause, Clinton gambled that Washington could not allow the British to threaten the complex of fortifications at West Point and disrupt the flow of supplies and reinforcements from New England. Clinton was no stranger to the Highlands, having successfully advanced north towards Albany in October 1777, capturing Forts Montgomery and Clinton along the way in a failed attempt to reach Lieutenant General John Burgoyne's doomed column.

Clinton was correct in his assessment that Washington feared the loss of the West Point forts and the Highlands. Yet as much as West Point meant to the American cause, Washington also had a clearheaded understanding that the survival of the Continental Army trumped all other considerations. Throughout the war Washington exhibited a reticence to commit his army on terms he found to his disadvantage but at times exhibited flashes of a more aggressive spirit. This aggressive trait revealed itself throughout the course of the war and was typically tempered by the more cautious attitudes of members of his general staff. Washington's decision to attack Stony Point, in the face of widespread skepticism from his staff, was born of that spirit.

Washington found in Brigadier General Anthony Wayne a kindred spirit. Although Wayne had at times fallen into line with his fellow generals to support a more conservative approach, more often Washington had Wayne's support for more aggressive actions. Like Clinton, Wayne, in command of the American assault on Stony Point, would craft plans reflecting his own experience. Only two years earlier in September, 1777 Wayne had watched helplessly as his Pennsylvania division suffered through the trauma of a British night assault on his camp at Paoli. From that night at Paoli Wayne understood risks and rewards associated with the plan to attack Stony Point. Washington, Clinton, and Wayne would carry these experiences with them into the Hudson Highlands in 1779.

1

Stalemate, 1779

1779 began with high expectations for both American and British armies, which stood like two bloodied boxers responding to the bell to begin the next round, well into their fight, warily eyeing their opponents, both staggered from previous blows, both circling their opponents, waiting for an opportunity to strike.

General George Washington, Detroit Publishing Co., 1900 (Library of Congress).

In late December, 1778 American commander-in-chief George Washington was called to Philadelphia to discuss strategy for the coming year with members of a special Committee of Conference appointed from the Continental Congress. Although he entered the city on 22 December, Washington's arrival was formally announced to the general public on Christmas Eve when the *Pennsylvania Packet* published the announcement;

On Tuesday last arrived here, George Washington, esquire, Commander in Chief of the Armies of the United States. Too great for pomp and as if fond of the plain and respectable rank of a free and independent Citizen, His Excellency came in so late in the day as to prevent the Philadelphia Troop of Militia Light-Horse, Gentlemen, Officers of the Militia, and others of this city from shewing those marks of unfeigned regard for this GOOD and GREAT MAN.[1]

Washington began the discussions with Congress of future actions at the conclusion of a year that had witnessed a revival of American fortunes. Key to increased optimism among members of Congress was the treaty recently concluded with France, which promised to provide material and military assistance and appeared to open up new opportunities to defeat the British.

---

1   *Pennsylvania Packet, or the General Advertiser*, 24 December, 1778.

The conclusion of a formal alliance with France had also fundamentally altered British war policy. In May 1778, Sir Henry Clinton, the newly appointed commander of British forces in America, received two dispatches from Lord George Germain, principal secretary of state for American affairs. The first, dated 8 March 1778 was written prior to the British government learning of the French alliance with the Americans. The 21 March 1778 directive immediately superseded the previous missive and included a wide ranging change in government policy. The dispatch directed Clinton to take specific actions designed to protect British interests in light of the new reality of a French alliance with the Americans. Although modified and adjusted in the coming years, the core principles laid down in the 21 March directive formed the foundation of British military strategy in America for the remainder of the war.

Sir Henry Clinton: Portrait by John Smart (Public Domain)

Clinton was ordered to evacuate Philadelphia and withdraw to New York. In something of a panic Germain raised the possibility that unfolding events might require that New York also be evacuated, leaving a garrison at Rhode Island and moving the army to Canada. Clinton initially accepted that possibility, but calculated that in the event New York was evacuated Rhode Island would also have to be abandoned. In the interim Clinton was directed to dispatch troops north to Canada to reinforce existing garrisons in Nova Scotia and Newfoundland, and to send contingents to Bermuda and West Florida. In addition to dispatching these forces Clinton was to organize two expeditions. The smaller effort, requiring several thousand troops, was to be directed towards securing Georgia and South Carolina. More troubling was the directive to dispatch 5,000 men to attack French possessions in the Caribbean. This expedition, requiring the detachment of ten regiments under the command of Major General James Grant, significantly reduced Clinton's available forces and his ability to challenge Washington's Continental Army.

In addition to the new orders from Germain, representatives of the British government, the Earl of Carlisle, William Eden, and George Johnstone arrived in Philadelphia armed with authority to conclude a peace treaty with the rebellious Americans. The Carlisle Commission was prepared to concede all American demands short of full independence. Emboldened by the French Alliance the Continental Congress adopted a resolution in April 1778, pledging not to enter into any agreement that did not result in an independent United States and the departure of all British troops. While chances for success of the Carlisle Commission were always doubtful, the imminent withdrawal of the British Army from Philadelphia further diminished its prospects. The Commission retired to New York and spent the next five months unsuccessfully trying to complete their charge.

In accordance with Germain's directive Clinton evacuated Philadelphia in June 1778, pursued closely by Washington's army. At Monmouth Courthouse on 28 June 1778, Clinton turned on his pursuer, checking the American army and allowing the British army, Loyalists refugees and baggage to reach the safety of New York. Both Washington and Clinton could claim success at Monmouth. British forces displayed their usual aggressiveness and tactical finesse, driving back in confusion a disjointed American attack. Alternatively,

Washington's men, even in retreat, showed no signs of panic but rather a resilience and tenacity that reflected the rigorous training they had received the previous winter at Valley Forge under the program developed by Major General Baron Frederick Von Steuben.

Clinton bristled at the claims of Major General Charles Lee, repeated widely in subsequent press accounts, that the British had suffered 'a handsome check', writing that:

> [T]he rear guard of the King's army is attacked on its march by the avant garde of the enemy. It turns upon them, drives them back to their gross, remains some hours in their presence until all its advanced elements return, and then falls back, without being followed, to the ground from which the enemy had been first driven, where it continues for several hours undisturbed, waiting for the cool of the evening to resume its march.[2]

The impact of the French alliance had long reaching impacts on British strategy, as evidenced by Germain's directives to Clinton. In addition to providing needed supplies and financing to the Americans cause, French involvement exponentially complicated British strategy. Not knowing where the French would strike at British interests, rather than being able to concentrate their efforts solely against Washington's army, British resources now had to be allocated to protect an area stretching from Canada to the West Indies. As Clinton duly organized the expedition to the West Indies he further reduced his New York garrison by dispatching four regiments to buttress the British defenses at Newport, Rhode Island.

British fears about French intervention were realized in July, 1778 when a French fleet under the command of Charles Hector, Comte d'Estaing, with 4,000 troops arrived off the American coast. While Washington favored a combined naval and land attack on New York, French concerns about the feasibility of crossing the shallow water between Sandy Hook and Staten Island resulted in a decision to attack the British at Newport, Rhode Island.

Awaiting the outcome of the offensive at Rhode Island, Washington moved the main American Army, numbering 20,000, to White Plains, north of New York in Westchester County. Situated above of the British positions at Kingsbridge, New York, Washington put the Continental Army in a position to react to circumstances as they developed at Rhode Island. Kingsbridge was a strategic position where the main post roads from Boston and Albany crossed the Spuyten Duyvil Creek, which separated Manhattan from the Bronx. As the northernmost British outpost it was heavily fortified to protect against American attack.

Clinton and Washington found themselves in a relative stalemate. Repeating his practice used during the June 1778 Monmouth campaign, Washington issued orders on 8 August 1778 to reassemble the ad hoc grouping of 'picked men' referred to in various documents as 'light infantry' to harass the British:

---

2   Clinton, Henry (ed. William Willcox), *The American Rebellion: Sir Henry Clinton's Narrative of His Campaigns, 1775-1782, with an Appendix of Original Documents* (New Haven, Connecticut: Yale University Press, 1954), p.97.

For the safety and ease of the Army and to be in greater readiness to attack or repel the Enemy, the Commander in Chief for these and many other Reasons orders and directs a Corps of Light Infantry composed of the best, most hardy and active Marksmen and commanded by good Partisan Offices be draughted from several Brigades to be commanded by Brigadier General Scott.[3]

At the same time Clinton organized a mixed force of Hessian *Jagers* and Loyalist provincial units to counter Scott's light infantry and patrol the neutral area between the two armies. These actions by both sides initiated a period of low-intensity warfare between the Americans and British, characterized by ambushing patrols and foraging parties and raiding outposts.

The joint Franco-American campaign against the British position at Newport, Rhode Island was hampered by poor communications and mutual distrust. The appearance of a British fleet resulted in French Vice Admiral Charles Hector d'Estaing abandoning the siege in early August, 1778 to engage the British fleet. After inconclusive maneuvering a storm scattered both the French and British fleets and d'Estaing retired to refit in Boston. American Major General John Sullivan, commander of the Continental army in Rhode Island, was infuriated, but could do nothing but complain bitterly to Washington and the Continental Congress. With the French withdrawal the British were able to regain the initiative. Sensing an opportunity to inflict a major defeat on Sullivan's army, Clinton quickly assembled at strong force of 4,000 men under Major General Charles Grey to relieve the besieged British garrison at Newport. The British garrison, commanded by Major General Robert Pigot, was alerted by deserters to a possible American withdrawal from their siege lines around Newport. When the Sullivan ordered the withdrawal on 28 August, Pigot ordered the British to pursue the Americans. Sullivan's force successfully withdrew, occupying a strong defensive position in the center of the island, and were able to repel a determined British attack on 29 August. Both sides suffered more than 200 casualties. Sullivan then successfully withdrew his army to Bristol, leaving the British in control of Aquidneck Island. Grey's relief force arrived on 1 September to find their quarry gone.

While he was trying to tap down the hostile reaction resulting from the decision of d'Estaing to abandon Sullivan's attack on the British at Rhode Island, Washington scheduled a Council of War on 1 September, inviting all major generals and brigadier generals to attend. The purpose of the Council was to discuss possible strategies in response to the unfolding events in Rhode Island. Washington laid out for his officers a summary of the current situation, with the French fleet at Boston, Sullivan's army under attack by the British, and a British relief force sailing from New York to Newport. Washington informed the officers that with the detachment of Grey's relief force the British had approximately 9,000 men remaining in New York, while the Continental Army, concentrated around White Plains, totaled approximately 12,700 men. Washington then presented the officers with several questions for their consideration. Washington wanted their opinions as to whether the army or some portion of it should undertake

---

3 'General Orders, 8 August 1778', *Founders Online,* National Archives.

offensive operations towards Rhode Island and if so, how should the Hudson Highlands be protected. Alternatively he held out the option of attacking New York, with its garrison temporarily depleted.

Over the next several days the officers sent back their opinions. The responses to the options outlined by Washington were uniformly skeptical of the success of possible attacks on Boston or Rhode Island, although several unenthusiastically acknowledged that if Sullivan's army was in danger of being overwhelmed by the British then Washington should march to its relief. As a group they were equally opposed to a possible attack on British lines around Kingsbridge or New York. Several pointed out the British enjoyed a distinct advantage provided by the Royal Navy, giving them the ability to move quickly to respond to threats around New York. The difficulties and possible cost of assaulting the strong British defensive positions at Kingsbridge were also mentioned. They observed that even if the Continentals were successful in capturing the Kingsbridge positions, or even penetrating the defenses of New York, Washington did not have the strength or resources to occupy them for any length of time.

Also of note is the response of Brigadier General Anthony Wayne to Washington's question concerning the possibility of an attack on the British lines at Kingsbridge. While his opinions concerning American attacks towards Boston or Rhode Island were consistent with the responses from other officers, Wayne was far more enthusiastic in his support of the action against Kingsbridge, writing, 'I am therefore clearly of Opinion that we should Remain in this Camp & take the first Opening to Strike the Enemy in the Vicinity of Kings Bridge, the mode & manner of this Attempt your Excellency will best Determine'.[4]

Despite the pessimism of most of his senior generals, Washington and his staff developed a plan for attacking the British strongpoints near Kingsbridge. Although the full text of the final plan for the attack has been lost, some of the key details are known. The plan appears to have anticipated a coordinated attack on British positions, included the use of detachments of light infantry under Brigadier Generals Charles Scott and Anthony Wayne. The attacks were to be supported by elements of the main army to surprise the British and Hessian defenders of Fort Knyphausen and numerous smaller forts and redoubts near Kingsbridge.

While the plan was never implemented – in part due to the lack of enthusiasm among his senior staff but more probably as a result of the quickly developing threat to Boston – the general outline provides insights into Washington's thinking about the assaulting fixed positions, including the use of light troops to conduct nighttime surprise attacks. Washington would return to these elements in the development of the plan for attacking Stony Point. While Washington may have been disappointed in the lack of aggressiveness displayed by most of his senior officers, Wayne's willingness to support a strike at the British was not lost on the American commander and would be remembered when the next opportunity presented itself.

Disappointed at missing their opportunity to trap Sullivan Clinton sailed to New London, Connecticut, where he initially intended to raid the town

---

4   Wayne to Washington, 2 September 1778, *Founders Online,* National Archives.

which was a center of privateering. A delay in the movement of the troop transports frustrated Clinton's plan and he dispatched Grey to continue towards Massachusetts while he returned to New York. Grey attacked New Bedford and Martha's Vineyard. Beginning on 4 September, Grey systematically pillaged New Bedford, burning ships, destroying warehouses and wharves and devastating the village. A detachment of British troops dispatched on 6 September to raid nearby Fairhaven was driven off by a growing force of local militia after destroying several buildings. Turning towards the island of Martha's Vineyard, contrary winds delayed Grey's sailing until 10 September. On 11 September the British sailed into Holmes Hole harbor and Grey issued an ultimatum to the local population, requiring surrender of all weapons and demanding the delivery stocks of cattle and sheep. Despite delays in assembling the livestock, which resulted in Grey threatening to ravage the community, the British sailed to New York on 15 September with 300 cattle and over 10,000 sheep.

With the news of Grant's attacks on Connecticut, New Bedford, and Martha's Vineyard Washington became uneasy about the possibility of an attack on the French fleet and detachment at Boston. Major General William Heath, writing from Boston on 15 September, reflected the concern of local officials that Boston was the next target, 'I think the Enemy are meditating mischief this way'.[5] As a precaution Washington issued orders on 15 September for the Continental Army to redeploy in response to the possible threat to Boston, but still be able to protect the Hudson Highlands. He assigned Major General Israel Putnam's three Virginia brigades to take up positions new near West Point, while two brigades under Brigadier General De Kalb were ordered to Fishkill. Lord Sterling's command of five brigades, along with Brigadier General Henry Knox's artillery, was deployed near Fredericksburg and Major General Horatio Gates' three brigades were joined by Major General Alexander McDougall's two brigades at Danbury. Scott's mixed force of light infantry and cavalry were ordered to retire a shorter distance and continue to maintain contact with the British around Kingsbridge to gather intelligence and harass foraging parties.

Major General Sullivan wrote Washington on 16 September from Providence, Rhode Island, convinced that the British 'may Either try for Boston & the French Fleet or evacuate America altogether, although I rather incline to the former'.[6] Washington had held out the possibility of a British evacuation of New York in his orders to Brigadier General Scott, advising him to immediately secure whatever supplies might be left behind. Washington's anxiety about Boston was relieved with a note from Major Genera Nathanael Greene, writing from Boston where he was securing supplies and acting as a liaison with the French forces. 'I can hardly think they mean to make an attempt upon Boston notwithstanding the object is important'.[7]

Grey returned to New York on 17 September and completely disembarked his captured livestock and the troops by 19 September. American fears about Boston were not completely unwarranted. Clinton, knowing he would have

---

5   Heath to Washington, 15 September 1778, *Founders Online*, National Achieves.
6   Sullivan to Washington, 16 September 1778, *Founders Online*, National Achieves.
7   Greene to Washington, 16 September 1778, *Founders Online*, National Achieves.

to detach significant forces to the West Indies and Georgia in the coming months, offered to accompany Vice Admiral Richard Lord Howe with 6,000 men to attack Boston. Howe, who was soon to relinquish command of the British naval forces in America to Vice Admiral John Byron, declined the offer and Clinton turned his attention back to New York.

During the early morning of 22 September 1778 the cream of the British army, totaling over 6,000 men, was transported from Red Hook, Brooklyn to Paulus Hook, New Jersey. The next day this force advanced north to New Bridge while the mixed force of Provincial light infantry and cavalry, followed by several Hessian brigades, pushed north from Kingsbridge to keep pace with Clinton's forces west of the Hudson River. In addition to attempting to goad Washington into making a strategic mistake, the British move into New Jersey served Clinton's need to gather substantial forage to support his forces in New York and the forces he was detaching to the Southern colonies and Caribbean.

Throughout the remainder of September and into early October the British reinforced their positions on both sides of the Hudson while continuing to collect forage. While Washington watched in frustration as the British stripped the New Jersey countryside of supplies he remained vigilant, encouraging Scott's detachment to gather intelligence. American efforts to gather information were further diminished when a force of British light infantry, grenadiers, regulars, and cavalry under General Charles Grey, returned from his expedition to Newport, surprised Colonel George Baylor's 3rd Continental Light Dragoon Regiment in the early morning of 28 September 1778 near Old Tappan, New Jersey, killing, wounding, or capturing approximately 60 cavalrymen.

While the British appeared to be getting the better of the skirmishes in Westchester and Bergen Counties, contact with British forces did produce useful intelligence. Washington took note of the information from a steady stream of British deserters that Clinton was about to dispatch ten regiments to the West Indies and the related detachment of smaller forces to Canada and the southern colonies. Washington recognized that the dispatch of forces from New York reduced Clinton's freedom of action in the coming year but, unlike many in Congress and the public, was skeptical that these moves portended a general British evacuation of New York.

On 28 September 1778 Clinton continued to keep Washington off balance by ordering a mixed force of Provincial and British troops, under the command of Captain Patrick Ferguson, to raid the American privateer base at Egg Harbor, New Jersey. At Egg Harbor the American had established a large salt works and naval depot used to supply privateers. After battling contrary winds for several days the task force arrived at its destination on 5 October 1778 and began a series of incursions, destroying the supply depot and salt works. On 15 October 1778 Ferguson's men surprised Count Casimir Pulaski's Legion near Egg Harbor during an early morning attack reminiscent of Grey's attack on Baylor at Old Tappan. Betrayed by several deserters, Pulaski's Legion suffered severe losses as Ferguson's men swept unhindered into their camp, bayoneting the sleeping and disoriented Legionaries.

Clinton began withdrawing British forces in Westchester County on 10 October, 1778. Bad weather helped screen the British withdrawal from the continued probes of American light infantry and cavalry. In Bergen County, British forces under the command of Lieutenant General Lord Cornwallis also completed their collection of forage and destroyed the fortifications built to protect their positions as they prepared to withdraw. Over the next two weeks the British retired in phases, reoccupying their former positions around New York. Ferguson's successful expedition returned to New York on 24 October 1778 bringing in additional supplies. Clinton finalized the implementation of the directives from Germain, detaching several regiments for Nova Scotia and West Florida at the end of October 1778. The largest detachment bound for the West Indies, under Major General James Grant, sailed on 3 November1778 followed by a smaller force destined for Georgia.

British Commodore William Hotham transported Grant's men first to Barbados, arriving on 10 December 1778, where they were joined by Rear Admiral Samuel Barrington. The combined force then sailed to St. Lucia and Grant landed a force on 13 December 1778, capturing the capital Castries the next day. Barrington's naval forces defeated the French fleet under d'Estaing on 15 December 1778 while British troops repulsed repeated French attacks at the Battle of Vigie on 18 December 1778. The French evacuated the island on 28 December 1778.

The Georgia expedition, led by Lieutenant Colonel Archibald Campbell with 3,500 men, was ordered to capture Savannah, a major seaport on the Georgia coast. Campbell's force arrived off the coast of Georgia on 23 December 1778. On 28 December 1778, Campbell's forced sailed up the Tybee River to land within three miles of Savannah. The next day, with the aid of loyalist guides, Campbell's force approached the town through the surrounding swamps, surprising and overwhelming the American garrison, commanded by Major General Robert Howe.

With the British withdrawal from Westchester and Bergen Counties, and the dissolution of his forces through the dispatch of expeditions to the fringes of Britain's North American holdings, Clinton found himself back in New York wondering how best he could pursue the war with Washington with fewer resources than he had available several months before. Although the continued assistance of the British fleet ensured his position in New York was secure, his failure to force Washington's army into a decisive engagement meant the war would continue into the new year.

In mid-November Colonel David Henley took over command of the Light Corps from Brigadier General Scott. As a result of several months of desultory skirmishing, the men and officers of the American light infantry had gained additional confidence and experience, despite being regularly outmaneuvered by their British opponents. On 25 November 1778 Washington notified his senior staff to begin preparations for distributing the army into winter quarters, effectively ending the campaigning season. Specific orders were issued on 27 November directing the deployment of American divisions at Danbury, Connecticut; in the vicinity of West Point; Albany, New York; and Middlebrook, New Jersey. Washington ordered Colonel Henley to disband the Light Corps and return the men to their parent units at their winter quarters. Washington himself joined his forces at Middlebrook.

2

Washington, Clinton, and their Plans

With his army dispersed into winter quarters, Washington turned his attention to responding to an ongoing discussion with members of the Continental Congress about options for pursuing the war in 1779. Similar to the examination of options he initiated with his own staff and generals Washington was prepared to explore a range of options with a Congressional committee. However, before addressing the most immediate problem of what to do about the continued British occupation of New York and Rhode Island, Washington needed to respond to a Congressional plan to invade Canada.

In early September 1778 Washington appointed a panel composed of Major General Horatio Gates, Brigadier General Jacob Bayley, and Colonel Moses Hazen, to advise him on the feasibility of invading Canada. All three officers were veterans of the Saratoga campaign that led to the surrender of Lieutenant General John Burgoyne's army, and familiar with the strategic challenges of operating along the Canadian border. The group pointed out that there were several different routes apart from Lake Champlain available to an American invading force and that much depended on the strength and disposition of British forces in Canada. If the British were not significantly reinforced, the group believed a winter campaign, beginning in January, would be feasible. Alternatively, if British strength increased, the winter option would be precluded but a summer campaign, begun in July or August, could be undertaken. Either option would require adequate supplies, oxen able to pull wagons or sleds in the winter, and that supplies were plentiful along the Connecticut River settlements. The panel's report focused primarily on supply availability and did not address more strategic considerations.

Washington passed along the findings of the panel to Henry Laurens, President of the Continental Congress, on 12 September 1778. In transmitting the report Washington pointed out that British naval superiority on the lakes prohibited their use and that much depended on whether the British withdrew from the colonies and to what degree they reinforced their Canadian forces. If the British were to 'keep their present footing, we shall find

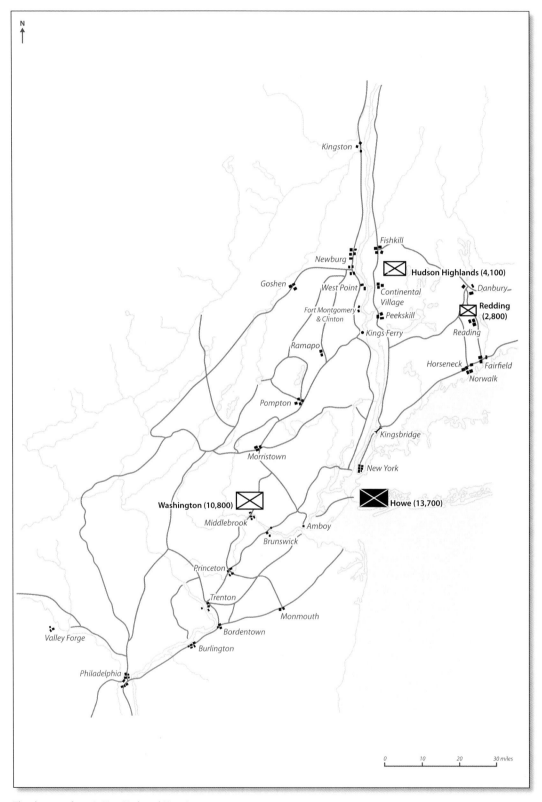

The theater of war in New York and New Jersey.

employment enough in defending ourselves, without mediating conquests; or if they send a large addition of strength into that country, it may require greater force and more abundant supplies on our part, to effect its reduction, than our resources may perhaps admit.[1] Washington's note of transmittal tried to provide proper perspective to the Congressmen in hopes that they would appreciate the logistical and manpower challenges associated with an invasion. At the same time Washington instructed Brigadier General Bayley to make a concerted effort to collect a wide range of detailed intelligence on British military dispositions, the current state of the civil administration, the status of Canadian militia, and sentiments of the population towards the United States.

After receiving Washington's report Congress appeared undeterred at the challenges identified in the analysis, referring the report to the Committee on Foreign Affairs to continue conversations with representatives of the French court. The conquest of Canada represented an irresistible fascination for some members of the Congress, extending back to the beginning of the rebellion. In 1775 Congress ordered an invasion of Canada which ended in failure but the prospect of incorporating Canada as the 14th colony, while dim, did not disappear. Although the strategic situation between the British and Continental armies remained largely unchanged, for many in Congress the treaty with France opened up a wide range of new possibilities. Rather than be seen as a cautionary note for future endeavors the missteps at Rhode Island between the French and Continentals seems to have been summarily dismissed as the Committee on Foreign Affairs moved forward in preparing their plan.

Washington responded on 25 September to Major General the Marquis de Lafayette concerning prospects for a Canadian invasion. Lafayette, who had tentatively been tapped to lead the invasion, requested Washington's opinion on how best to proceed. Washington counseled Lafayette that he should proceed with his plans to travel to France over the winter rather than postpone his trip on the expectation that the proposed invasion might require his participation

Between the receipt of Washington's report and the end of October the Committee developed a detailed plan, which was reviewed on 22 October and submitted to Washington for his review on 27 October. Without waiting for Washington's reaction Congress referred the plan to Benjamin Franklin, head of the American delegation to France, on 28 October 1778, and directed it be presented to the French Court for their consideration. Washington was also directed to gather intelligence on British dispositions in Canada and make that information available to the French. Lafayette was assigned to carry the plan to Franklin in France.

The plan envisioned a multi-pronged effort to attack the British at Detroit and advance to Niagara, engaging the Seneca and other Indian tribes as necessary. At the same time an American force of approximately 5,000 men was to be directed to move north towards the St. Lawrence, attacking Montreal and St. John's. After securing navigation of Lake Ontario the American forces were to advance against Quebec.

---

1   Washington to Laurens, 12 September 1778, *Founders Online*, National Achieves.

French cooperation was considered essential and the plan identified French interests in acquiring access to the Newfoundland fishery and Quebec as well as suggesting that the weakening of the British position in North America would pay dividends in the struggle against the British in the West Indies. The plan proposed that a force of 5,000 French sail in May 1779 and, in conjunction with American troops, capture Quebec and Montreal. Once resupplied the combined force would proceed to capture Halifax in September or October. If successful and the season not too far advanced, Newfoundland could then be occupied. If Halifax could not be captured the plan suggested the French squadron and troops could proceed to the West Indies and return the following year to complete the conquest.

The plan was forwarded to Washington for his review and comment, as was a request to collect information on British dispositions in Canada that would be forwarded to the French. Washington wrote to Henry Laurens on 11 November 1778 providing a measured but comprehensive critique of the proposed plan. Washington began by affirming that his support for the 'emancipation of Canada as an Object very interesting to the future prosperity and tranquility of these States', but having established that the conquest of Canada was a laudable goal he proceeded to systematically dismantle each of the key elements of the plan. Washington noted that it would be 'impolitic' to propose a course of action to the French 'without a moral certainty of being able to fulfill our part, particularly if the first proposal came from us'.[2] He suggested that the plan misappropriated limited military and naval resources that could be utilized in other enterprises and that could be ill afforded to be lost if the effort failed.

Washington pointed out that as long as the British occupied both New York and Rhode Island he would be unable to justify the diversion of resources to the proposed Canadian invasion. He duly noted there was no hard evidence that the British were preparing to abandon either position and that he would continue to require 12,000 to 15,000 men to protect the colonies from incursions from either garrison while observing that the invasion plan as proposed would require more than 12,000 additional men.

Washington questioned the ability of the colonies to procure adequate supplies for both the standing army and the invasion force, which would include not only a significant French infantry contingent but also naval resources. He was also dismissive of the proposed role of American militia in the overall enterprise, observing that 'militia have neither patience nor perseverance for a siege … an attempt to carry One, which would materially depend on them, would be liable to be frustrated, by their inconsistency'. Washington questioned the assumption implicit in the proposed plan that the British would remain passive in the face of the possible loss of her Canadian possessions, writing 'I should apprehend we may run into a dangerous error by estimating her power so low'.[3] He told Congress that the British would invariably learn the details of the proposed invasion and respond accordingly by reinforcing their garrisons at Montreal and Quebec, further complicating American efforts. Alternatively he pointed out that if

---

2   Washington to Laurens, 11 November 1778, *Founders Online,* National Archives.
3   Washington to Laurens, 11 November 1778, *Founders Online,* National Archives.

the British evacuated New York or Rhode Island these troops would be used to reinforce the Canadian garrisons. He dismissed the practical impact of the French naval forces, maintaining that British naval superiority would not affected and that if the French fleet was either defeated or scattered by a storm the invasion force would be at great risk. He acknowledged that the inclusion of the Spanish fleet could tip the balance but was pessimistic that Spain would declare support for the American cause in the near term.

In the end Washington concluded 'The plan proposed appears to me not only too extensive and beyond our abilities, but too complex. To succeed it requires such a fortunate coincidence of circumstances, as could hardly be hoped, and cannot be relied on'.[4] That the plan was ambitious was obvious, but Congress believed the specter of reacquiring Canadian possessions would be enticing enough to allay any reservations the French might have. In a similar manner in addition to operational and logistical problems Washington harbored serious concerns about the potential intentions of France if they agreed to the invasion.

In a private letter to Henry Laurens on 14 November 1778 Washington raised an 'objection to it [the invasion] untouched in my public letter'. Stated simply, Washington was fearful that the presence of 5,000 or more French troops in Canada and possession of Quebec would be 'too great a temptation' and would lead to a reestablishment of French control over Canada rather than the integration of Canada into the newly created United States. While Washington believed that the French might agree to enter into the proposed expedition with the purist of intentions 'no Nation is to be trusted farther than it is bound by its interests, And no prudent Statesman or politician will venture to depart from it'.[5]

Accordingly on 5 December 1778 Washington's response was referred to a Congressional committee of conference. The resolution recognized Washington's concerns and noted that success of the proposed enterprise would depend on a substantial commitment from the French. An 18 December 1778 resolution requested that Washington meet with the Committee once the army was settled in winter quarters.

Washington arrived in Philadelphia on the evening of 22 December 1778 and was officially received by Congress on 24 December 1778, beginning a series of meeting with a committee of conference composed of James Duane, Jesse Root, Meriwether Smith, Gouverneur Morris, and Henry Laurens that would last until early February 1779. Washington notified Lafayette by letter on 29 December 1778 that plans for the Canadian invasion had been shelved indefinitely, wishing him a safe trip to France.

With the Canadian project sidelined Washington set about outlining his assessment of future options with the Congressional Committee of Conference. As he was preparing a summary of options for the committee Washington asked Major General Nathanael Greene for his thoughts on the coming campaign. Writing on 5 January 1779 Greene identified three primary objectives that should guide Washington's actions.

---

4   Washington to Laurens, 11 November 1778, *Founders Online,* National Archives.
5   Washington to Laurens, 14 November 1778, *Founders Online,* National Archives.

Greene believed it was essential that the main army take up positions that ensured it could be efficiently supplied and concluded that New Jersey met that criteria. He recognized that strong detachments, representing perhaps one third of available manpower, would be needed in the Hudson Highlands to maintain communications with the New England states and in Connecticut to respond to possible British incursions. He also suggested a force of men be dispatched in June to the western frontier to drive off the Indian tribes and destroy their crops. Finally he held out the possibility of an attack on New York itself but cautioned that this effort would depend on the possible reduction in the British garrison and would require a feint against Rhode Island in order to limit the possible transfer of reinforcements from that garrison.

Washington's lengthy missive to the committee of 13 January 1779 reflected this same thinking but also addressed equally important administrative issue such as bounty's to encourage both recruitment and reenlistments. Washington laid out three possible dispositions in the coming year, all based on the premise that the British would continue to hold their current positions.

The first option would commit the American army to expel the British from New York and Rhode Island. Washington readily admitted that this was the most preferable option but, given the strength of British fortifications, could only be undertaken if the American army was substantially increased. He estimated a minimum of 26,000 men would be necessary to undertake this offensive and raised serious doubt that an army of that size could be readily supplied.

The second option was to initiate the conquest of Canada while remaining on the defensive before New York and Rhode Island. Washington concluded that a minimum of 13,000 men would be necessary to remain opposite New York and Rhode Island, while a force totaling at least 20,000 would be needed to invade Canada. He pointed out that this option would be more expensive than the first option and pose even more troublesome logistical problems to adequately maintain the armies.

By default Washington concluded that the third option, for the American army to remain on the defensive, was the most feasible. While the main army adopted a defensive posture Washington allowed that an expedition against the Indians on the frontier should also be undertaken. Washington felt this option would allow the Americans to repair their finances, which would allow for a more predictable flow of supplies. This pause would also allow the army to continue to restructure and provide more time to train. Washington recognized this defensive posture would be interpreted as a sign of weakness, which would work against inducing Spain or other European nations from declaring their support for the United States. Domestically the inaction of the army would dispirit patriots and give encouragement to Loyalists.

Although Washington recommended the third option, he held out the possibility that, if the British were to evacuate their positions in New York and Rhode Island, efforts could be initiated to undertake the Canadian invasion. Towards that end, while he issued orders ending general preparations for the Canadian expedition he directed Major General Nathanael Greene to continue efforts underway to construct galleys and bateaux.

Washington's recommendation for caution was bolstered with news on 20 January 1779 that the British had captured Savannah. Having been absent from the army for over a month, Washington requested permission to rejoin his men. Permission being granted, Washington returned to Middlebrook on 5 February 1779. He was still at a loss to discern Clinton's intentions for the coming campaign. Writing a letter of appreciation to Henry Laurens on 17 February 1779 for the hospitality shown to him and his wife Martha during their recent stay in Philadelphia Washington noted that there was nothing new to report of the enemy but intimated he was aware that the signing of a treaty with Spain, that included a substantial loan, was close to being finalized. While he waited for events to clarify Clinton's intentions he spent his time overseeing an never ending series of squabbles over rank and promotion between officers and addressing administrative issues, courts-martial, supply distribution, and recruitment. During this period he was also deeply engaged in organizing the proposed expedition against the Indians along the frontier.

Washington also was engaged in establishing an early-warning system for militia in New Jersey. While he was skeptical of the long term military value of militia, reflected in his criticism of the reliance of the Congressional Canadian invasion plan on the assumption of participation of militia, Washington also recognized that the timely response of militia was essential to support the efforts of the Continental Army to respond to future British movements. In March, 1779 Washington wrote to several senior officers directing them to build a series of beacons on high ground that would be visible to the surrounding countryside. Washington's plan was the result of consultation with several militia officers and was based on their recommendations. The beacons were proposed to be constructed with logs in the form of a pyramid, 16 to 18 feet square at the base, 20 feet tall, filled with brush. The beacons would be set on fire to alert the militia to British movements and direct them to quickly assemble at designated locations. Washington's directive focused initially on specific locations that would support the Middlebrook encampment within Sommerset and Middlesex Counties. It was Washington's intention that this system of alerting militia would be expanded to other counties in New Jersey.

As Washington was dissuading Congress from pursuing the ill-advised invasion of Canada and cooperating with the Committee of Conference to develop a realistic strategy for the coming year, Lieutenant General Henry Clinton was trying to pick up the pieces after grudgingly fulfilling the directives from Lord Germain. In total Clinton had detached over 10,000 men, leaving him with an effective force of approximately 13,500 men. In late July 1778 Clinton had sent a dispatch to Germain suggesting that, given the reduction in his available forces, he might be forced to evacuate New York by the end of September 1778. Clinton's assessment of British options in the coming year identified two stark alternatives; undertaking offensive actions, which would require an infusion of significant additional resources, or abandoning their current positions and conducing raids on the Americans from strongholds in Canada and the West Indies.

Although Germain's dispatch of 21 March 1778 had recognized the real possibility of retreating to Canada, Clinton's September 1778 assessment dismissed that option as unnecessary and overly pessimistic. The sense of panic which had gripped the British government in early 1778 with confirmation of the French intervention had given way to an equally unrealistic optimism that Clinton could make due with available resources.

In clear frustration at the lack of resources and contrary instructions from Whitehall, Clinton forwarded a request on 8 October 1778 that the King relieve him of command. Germain responded on 3 December 1778 denying his request, while commending his zeal and reaffirming the King's confidence in his leadership. Other than the evacuation of Philadelphia and dispatch of the various expeditions included in the 21 March 1778 letter, Germain offered that 'the disposition and employment of the troops will be, as it was always intended they should be, left to your judgement'.[6] Germain concluded that the unfortunate directives included in the 21 March letter were necessitated by the entry of the French into the war and concern over the need to protect British possessions in the West Indies.

While fulminating against his circumstances, Clinton received information on 28 November 1778 from an American deserter that the British and German troops captured by the Americans at Saratoga – the Convention Army – were to be moved from Massachusetts to Charlottesville, Virginia. Clinton was also apprised of the detachment of a portion of Washington's army to western New York in response to the 11 November 1778 attack of Loyalists and Indians in the Cherry Valley. Clinton immediately dispatched a mixed force of cavalry, regulars, light infantry, and grenadiers under the command of Brigadier Generals Edward Mathew and Sir William Erskine to attempt to liberate the British prisoners. While portion of the force marched along the Hudson River to Tarrytown, the bulk of the British infantry traveled north by water. Contrary winds delayed the movement up the Hudson resulting in the British force missing their target by several days. As the weather was agreeable Clinton took the opportunity to land forces at Verplank's Point and Stony Point, along the Hudson River, to conduct a more complete reconnaissance of American dispositions. Clinton noted that both locations, which formed the terminals of the Kings Ferry, might prove useful in the future.

As he took stock of his situation in the early months of 1779 Clinton concluded that he had very few options available for a general offensive against Washington's army. Official returns for the British forces in American on 1 January 1779 included 16,600 effectives in and around New York, while almost 6,000 men were deployed at Rhode Island. In accordance with Germain's directive, Clinton organized hit and run expeditions intended to cripple American privateers and deny Washington needed supplies. The raids also provided an opportunity of capturing American troops who could then be exchanged for members of the captive British Convention Army. Clinton continued to look for opportunities to harass the Americans

---

6   Germain to Clinton, 3 December, 1778, Clinton, *The American Rebellion*, p.397.

using the superior mobility provided by the British Navy and information concerning the deployment of isolated American forces.

On 25 February 1779 Clinton dispatched a strong force of over 1,000 men under the command of Colonel Sterling to surprise American forces at Elizabethtown, New Jersey and attempt the capture of Governor William Livingston. The raid failed on both accounts, and after setting fire to several buildings and carrying off some supplies the British retired. A similar effort against Greenwich, New York produced similar results. In March 1779 Brigadier General Mathew was dispatched to attack the American shipping at Providence, Rhode Island. Despite having what was believed to be solid intelligence, Mathew's expedition found no ships at Providence and returned empty-handed.

Although Clinton maintained a realistic assessment of his ability to engage Washington in the coming year, the evolution of opinions at Whitehall, the seat of British government, were influenced by an unrealistic assessment of recent events. Despite their failure to secure engage the American Congress in meaningful discussions concerning the British proposals for ending the conflict the Carlisle Commission returned to England with news of discord in the American Congress and the continuing logistical and recruitment difficulties experienced by Washington's army. Coupled with the British success in capturing Savannah and subsequently reestablishing control over Georgia, and victories over the French in the West Indies, the British government grew more optimistic about the course of the war in America.

Beginning on 27 January 1779, Germain sent Clinton a litany of dispatches reflecting this newfound optimism. After Germain appeared to extend to Clinton total discretion in deciding how best to deploy his limited resources in his 3 December 1778 letter, Clinton was shocked and dismayed when he received, on 24 April 1779, the first in a series of long directives from Germain, written in January 1779, providing a specific outline for the military operations in the coming year and ordering that Clinton initiate offensive operations against the Americans, writing 'it is most earnestly to be wished that you may be able to bring Mr. Washington to a general and decisive action at the opening of the campaign.'[7] Failing that, Germain, who estimated that Clinton could deploy about 12,000 in the field, directed Clinton to force Washington's army either back into the Hudson Highlands or into New Jersey. In either case by doing so the Loyalists, whom the Carlisle Commission had convinced the British government were numerous and waiting to be rallied to the King's colors, would be free to reestablish British rule in New York.

In addition to attacking Washington's main army, Germain ordered Clinton to create two 4,000-man detachments, one to raid the New England coast while the other did the same in the Chesapeake Bay. Both were intended to attack American supply depots and privateer bases. Finally, writing that it 'surely is not too much to expect that your force will be so much increased by new levies, under the encouragement now given them, as to enable you to strengthen the corps you appoint to attack Virginia and Maryland', Germain ended his letter by promising Clinton approximately 6,600 additional men,

---

7   Germain to Clinton, 23 January, 1779, Clinton, *The American Rebellion*, p.398.

to arrive in the spring. In subsequent dispatches Germain also promised the return of Major General Grant's 5,000-strong detachment from the West Indies and informed Clinton that the King had accepted an offer from Lord Cornwallis to return to the America theater, appointing him second-in-command to Clinton.

In assessing the impact of Germain's directives Clinton estimated that, in order to maintain adequate garrisons at strategic locations and undertake the operations as ordered, he would need an army of at least 30,000, considerably more than his current strength of approximately 22,000. Whatever his reservations, Clinton dutifully began evaluating his options. Given his limited resources he determined to initiate a series of focused operations intended to support each other but dependent on the timely arrival of the promised reinforcements

Clinton's main challenge was how best to entice Washington to abandon his current deployment around Middlebrook and bring him to battle. Clinton determined that Washington's position at Middlebrook was too strong to challenge with his available forces. He briefly considered advancing his forces between Washington's army and American supply centers around Trenton and Princeton, New Jersey believing this might entice Washington to give battle. Clinton ultimately rejected that option believing it would put his army too far away from New York to ensure the safety of the garrison.

Clinton also considered dispatching Grant's forces south to capture Charleston, South Carolina but was doubtful that he could hold it for an extended period. He worried that an initial British success would encourage Loyalists to declare for the Crown, only to be abandoned to their rebel neighbors if his forces were forced to retire. Responding to a proposal from Commodore Sir George Collier, who now commanded British naval forces in North America, Clinton determined a raid into Virginia along the Chesapeake Bay should be attempted. Accordingly on 5 May 1779 Collier's ships sailed from Sandy Hook laden with British troops under the command of Edward Mathew, now a major general.

Clinton himself was a troubled man. Through April and May 1779 Clinton received a steady stream of letters apprising him of delays in the dispatch of promised reinforcements. Although Clinton appeared to have dutifully accepted the dramatic shifts in British strategy, he was becoming increasingly frustrated with the unfulfilled promises and unrealistic directives emanating from Whitehall. His initial response to the War Minister was tempered but direct. He reminded Germain of the obvious, noting that 'to force Washington to an action upon terms tolerably equal has been the object of every campaign during this war'. After noting that Washington had 8,000 Continental troops, more than his predecessor Howe had to face in 1777, Clinton dismissed Germain's suggestion that he drive Washington from his Middlebrook stronghold. Clinton proposed that 'it shall be my endeavor to draw Washington forward before he is Reinforced, by indirect Manouvres … to strike at him whilst he is in motion'.[8]

---

8   Clinton to Germain, 14 May 1779, quoted in Henry P. Johnson, *The Storming of Stony Point on the Hudson* (New York: White and Company, 1900), p.31

Clinton was particularly disgruntled by Germain's disingenuous promise to allow Clinton flexibility to conduct the was as he saw fit while at the same time issuing directives for specific actions, which required the allocation of limited resources. Clinton began his letter clarifying his expectations, writing 'when I was ordered to this difficult command … I was flattered with the hope of having every latitude allowed me to act as the moment should require'. With those expectations Clinton wondered, 'How mortified then must I be, My Lord, at finding movements recommended for my debilitated army which your Lordship never thought of suggesting to Sir William Howe when he was in his greatest force and without an apprehension from a foreign enemy!'[9]

As Clinton noted, 'I am on the spot; the earliest and most exact intelligence on every point ought naturally, from my situation, to reach me' pointing out the obvious advantage he had over Germain, to react quickly as information was received. Referring to the unrealistic assumptions upon which British ministers were making decisions, Clinton lamented, 'Why then, My Lord, without consulting me, will you adopt the ill-digested or interested suggestions of people who cannot be competent judges of the subject'. In evident frustration Clinton declared, 'For God's sake, my Lord, if you wish me to do anything, leave me to myself and let me adapt my effects to the hourly changes of circumstances'.[10]

Germain responded in an oblique manner, addressing a letter in June 1779 not to Clinton but to Major Duncan Drummond, Clinton's aide-de-camp. Germain began by admitting 'I have received letters from Sir Henry Clinton very different from those I expected'.[11] Germain assured Drummond that Clinton had been given maximum leeway to choose the proper course of action as he saw it. Germain pointed out that both he and Clinton were of the same mind as far as the attack on Georgia and the raids along the Chesapeake were concerned, and that Clinton would be given credit for all successes and Germain would support any decisions that resulted in a reverse. Germain also defended the conclusions of the Carlyle Commission that Loyalist sentiment was widespread and, if nurtured through British battlefield victories, would be decisive in returning the colonies to the King.

Having unburdened himself to Germain, Clinton turned his attention to finalizing the next step in his campaign to defeat Washington by bringing the Continental Army to a decisive battle.

9   Clinton to Germain, 22 May, 1779, Clinton, *The American Rebellion*, p.407.
10   Clinton to Germain, 22 May, 1779, Clinton, *The American Rebellion*, p.408.
11   Germain to Drummond, 23 June 1779, Clinton, *The American Rebellion*, p.409.

3

Strategic Considerations

As Clinton surveyed the stage on which he and Washington were to spar over the next several months there were several important strategic considerations that would limit his options and govern his next moves. There were two realities that he would also have to address: the strength of Washington's position at Middlebrook and the strategic value of the Hudson Highlands.

The American encampment at Middlebrook had already proven a thorn in the British side. In the aftermath of the battles of Trenton and Princeton in December 1776 and January 1777, Washington had settled the American army into winter quarters at Jockey Hollow, near Morristown, New Jersey. Washington had also assigned Benjamin Lincoln's brigade to remain at Boundbrook, south of Morristown, to observe the British detachment that occupied New Brunswick. Boundbrook was located just south of the Watchung Mountains, along the Raritan River. Lincoln's responsibility was to cover the key crossings of the Raritan River and provide early warning if the British advanced out of New Brunswick to attack the Morristown encampment. In that role Lincoln's men engaged British patrols and forage parties throughout the winter. Annoyed at the continuing presence of Lincoln's men Lieutenant General Lord Cornwallis organized an attack on Lincoln's position at Boundbrook. On 12 April, 1777 Cornwallis led 4,000 men out of New Brunswick to surprise Lincoln, whose strength had dwindled to just over 500 men due to expiring enlistments. Although Cornwallis failed to surround and capture Lincoln's entire force, the British did drive the Americans into a precipitous retreat, abandoning cannon and supplies, including Lincoln's personal papers. After the British withdrawal the next morning Washington reoccupied Boundbrook but the British attack highlighted its continued vulnerability.

At the end of May 1777, Washington establishing a camp just north of Boundbrook, on the Middlebrook heights, to observe British movements around New Brunswick and Perth Amboy, New Jersey. Located along the first range of the Watchung Mountains the Middlebrook location offered Washington several advantages. The sharply rising ground offered an ideal defensive position, from which American forces could monitor British movements out of nearby New Brunswick and react to any expeditions from New York. The road network serving Midddlebrook provided ready access to the American supply bases at Morristown and Princeton. In spring 1777, Washington responded to a Congressional Committee's recommendation that a portion of the Army be repositioned from Middlebrook to positions astride the Delaware River to protect Philadelphia. After describing the shortcomings of occupying positions closer to Philadelphia, Washington wrote 'I think it is plain, that we must establish a respectable Force where we now are, as the most convenient point, from whence we give opposition to the Enemy, should their designs be either Northward or Southward.'[1]

Clinton's predecessor, Lieutenant General William Howe, had tried without success in early June 1777 to draw Washington's army down from the Middlebrook position. On 12 June 1777 Howe advanced out of New Brunswick with 18,000 men but Washington refused to be drawn into battle. After Howe's retreat to Perth Amboy, Washington ordered his forces to follow the British and Brigadier General Lord Sterling's division was directed to the Scotch Plains area on the American left. Sensing an opportunity Howe turned and attacked Sterling's mixed division of 2,500 men on 26 June, 1777, attempting to overwhelm the smaller American force and cut off Washington from the Middlebrook defenses. Although driven back, Sterling's men put up a determined defense, allowing the main army to withdraw to Middlebrook, which Howe judged too strong to assault.

Unable to dislodge Washington from Middlebrook, Howe was reluctant to move his army overland in his advance to capture Philadelphia and so. rather than expose his movements to possible attack from the Americans at Middlebrook. he chose to utilize the fleet and move by water to Head of Elk, Maryland and then overland to Philadelphia. The additional time required for the combined operation guaranteed that Howe would be unable to support the advance of General Burgoyne's army from Canada towards Albany, New York. The failure of Burgoyne's offensive and eventual surrender at Saratoga, New York in October, 1777 represented a major setback for British strategy and paved the way for the American alliance with France.

Washington's familiarity with the Middlebrook position led him, in December 1777, to assign major elements of the American Army to the area. Infantry brigades from the Pennsylvania, Maryland, and Virginia, as well as the American artillery park, were deployed at Middlebrook. The troops began their winter encampment housed in tents but by the end of the winter had constructed sturdier log huts. Washington and his staff were housed in private homes scattered throughout the area. The winter of 1777-1778 was relatively mild, with little snow. Unlike the previous winter at Valley Forge, the troops were kept adequately supplied with food and received newly arrived uniforms of blue and brown from France.

Recognizing the strength of the Middlebrook position, General Clinton faced the same dilemma as Howe. With his limited resources assaulting the Middlebrook defenses was clearly not a realistic option, but given Howe's unsuccessful attempts to entice Washington out of Middlebrook in 1777 Clinton would have to find another way.

---

1   Washington to Robert Morris, George Clymer, and George Walton, 12 April 1777, *Founders Online,* National Archives.

The Hudson Highlands encompass a large area north of New York City, straddling the Hudson River, also referred as the North River. The Hudson River corridor was recognized by both Americans and British as the gateway to Canada. In addition, the ferry at Kings Ferry was a strategic connection between New England and the Middle Atlantic states, allowing for essential communications as well as the movement of necessary supplies and military units. In 1775 the Continental Congress encouraged the New York Provincial Convention to take steps to fortify the Highlands. The Provincial Convention dispatched several members who identified several possible locations for enhanced defenses, including Stony Point, Verplanck's Point and Martlaer's Rock, a small island near West Point, on which Fort Constitution was built.

John Adams highlighted the role of the Highlands in a 6 January 1776 letter to Washington, writing 'the North River which is in it [New York], in the progress of this War, as it is the Nexus of the Northern and Southern Colonies, as a King of Key to the whole Continent, as it is a Passage to Canada to the Great Lakes and to all the Indian Nations. No Effort to secure it should be omitted.' [2] Ongoing disputes about the location and design of potential fortifications frustrated attempts to strengthen the defenses in the Highlands, leading Washington to appoint Brigadier General William Alexander, Lord Sterling, to conduct a thorough survey of the Hudson. Sterling's recommendations included the need to fortify Stony Point and Verplanck's Point but surprisingly did not include mention of the West Point location. Work was begun on defenses at a number of other locations, including Popolopen Creek, which was named Fort Montgomery, the nearby Fort Clinton, and Anthony's Nose. In addition, a large chain, intended to block shipping, was deployed across the river between Fort Montgomery and Anthony's Nose.

In early 1777 Washington appointed Major General Israel Putnam to oversee the improvement of the defenses. He also appointed a committee led by Major General Nathanael Greene and included Brigadier Generals Henry Knox and Anthony Wayne to confirm the previous recommendations for fortifying the Highlands. While the Committee recommended minor modifications and improvements along the Hudson, the vulnerability of the forts to an overland attack overland from the west was overlooked.

Clinton's interest in the strategic potential of the Highlands to British war strategy began soon after his arrival in New York on 4 February, 1776. Clinton's discussions with Lord William Tyron, Governor of New York in the summer of 1776 Clinton's, focused on how best to dislodge the American forces from their positions on Manhattan. Beyond those immediate considerations Clinton identified the need to establish firm communications between British forces in New York and Canada He was aware that the Americans were already fortifying sections of the Hudson Highlands and thought it prudent to seize these areas before the defenses could be strengthened. Given his already strained relationship with Howe, Clinton let the idea drop.

Burgoyne's offensive from Canada in 1777 proved to confirm both Washington's and Clinton's worst fears about the importance of the Highlands. With the start of Burgoyne's invasion, Washington believed

---

2   Adams to Washington, 6 January 1776, *Founders Online*, National Archives.

Howe would strike north from New York towards Albany in support of Burgoyne. Accordingly Washington moved the American army north into the Highlands, positioning his forces along Smith's Clove, an key passage leading through the mountains on the west bank of the Hudson River. From Smith's Clove Washington was confident he could react quickly to whatever action Howe should take.

When he received word that Burgoyne had captured Fort Ticonderoga in July 1777, Howe assumed Burgoyne's offensive would have little difficulty capturing Albany. With that assumption Howe sailed out of New York on 23 July 1777 headed for Philadelphia. Washington, apprised of Howe's departure, followed him south from the Highlands. Although Howe had taken the bulk of the British Army with him as part of his offensive to capture Philadelphia, General Clinton was left in New York with a substantial garrison. Before leaving New York Howe left Clinton a series of instructions. In one, dated 9 July 1777 he affirmed that Clinton was to command all the troops in the New York region and any reinforcements that might arrive in his absence. He also told Clinton that he could 'make such changes in the position of them as you may judge most conducive to his Majesty's service for the defence of this important post.'[3]

Soon after sailing, almost as a postscript, Howe wrote Clinton on 30 July 1777 promising to send reinforcements when possible and noting, 'In the mean while, if you can make any diversion in favour of General Burgoyne's approaching Albany, with security to Kings Bridge, I need not point out the utility of such a measure.'[4]

With these instructions in hand a nervous Clinton informed Burgoyne that 'Sir W. Howe is gone to the Chesapeake bay with the greatest part of the army. I hear he is landed but am not certain. I am left to command here with too small a force to make any effectual diversion in your favour. I shall try something at any rate. It may be of use to you. I own to you I think Sir W.'s move just at this time the worst he could make.'[5]

Clinton received an upbeat message from Burgoyne, dated 5 August 1777 suggesting he was making good progress and anticipated being at Albany, New York by 25 August. By the end of the month Clinton had been received news of the British defeat at Bennington, Vermont but additional definitive information about Burgoyne's situation was scarce. Burgoyne's optimistic timetable proved incorrect as August turned to September. News that Burgoyne's army was stalled at Saratoga, 40 miles short of Albany, brought the onus of the campaign back to Clinton. Clinton's interpretation of Howe's instructions put a premium on safeguarding New York and any foray up into the Hudson Highlands could only be undertaken at the request of Burgoyne. Clinton wrote Burgoyne on 11 September suggesting he was planning on an attack against the American forts along the Hudson in ten days. Ironically Clinton's offer, which reached Burgoyne on 21 September, doomed his army

---

3   Howe to Clinton, 9 July 1777, quoted in William Howe, *The Narrative of Lieut. Gen Sir William Howe in a committee of the House of Commons* (London: H. Baldwin, 1780), p.22

4   Quoted in Howe, *Narrative*, p.23.

5   Quoted in Dave Richard Palmer, *The River and the Rock* (New York: Greenwood Publishing, 1969) p.94.

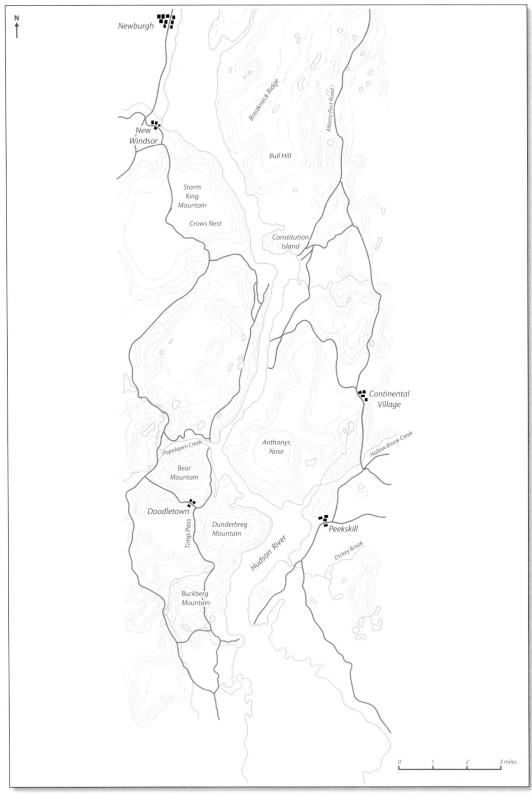

The Hudson Highlands.

by dissuaded him from renewing his attack on the American army barring his way to Albany. Burgoyne decided to wait in vain hope that Clinton's attack would draw off American forces, improving his odds of success when he renewed his attack.

On 29 September Clinton was emboldened by a response from Burgoyne that stated 'an attack or even the menace of one upon Fort Montgomery would be of great use to him.'[6] More importantly the courier provided Clinton with details of the dire straits of Burgoyne's force and Burgoyne's intention to force his way through the American army to Albany. Clinton was now prepared to act.

Clinton's options had been improved when on 24 September the long awaited reinforcements from England sailed into New York. The 1,700 British and Hessian recruits bolstered Clinton's available forces and allowed him to assign approximately 3,000 troops to the expedition into the Highlands. His plan included landing a force at Stony Point, which then was to move along the west side of the Hudson River and assault Fort Montgomery and Fort Clinton. To confuse Putnam about his ultimate intentions Clinton ordered another column to land on the east bank, at Verplanck's Point and appear to threaten the American supply base at Peekskill, New York. Putnam reacted as Clinton hoped, transferring troops towards Peekskill and reducing the garrisons of Forts Montgomery and Clinton to just 600 men.

Clinton's plan was put into action on 3 October, 1777 with the landing of the diversionary force at Verplanck's Point, followed on 6 October with the landing of the main force at Stony Point. Quickly splitting the Stony Point force into two columns the British forces captured the strategic Timp Pass and assaulted Forts Montgomery and Clinton from the land side. By the end of the day both forts had fallen and Clinton pushed further north, capturing Fort Constitution on 8 October, 1777. Clinton's forces quickly followed up their success by capturing American supplies at Continental Village and Fishkill.

As Clinton was transferring his forces to the west bank on 5 October a courier brought a startling message from Burgoyne announcing his supply lines to Canada were threatened and, although he still believed he could reach Albany, he needed Clinton's assurance his army could be supplied from New York. If he did not hear from Clinton by 12 October he would retreat across the lakes while he still believed he had time. Clinton sent Burgoyne news of his success on 8 October but could not guarantee his small command would be able to force its way to Albany.

Another message from Burgoyne arrived on 9 October with the same dire assessment of his situation but also requesting orders from Clinton on Howe's behalf. Clinton replied immediately that he had no authority to issue Burgoyne orders and that he would do what he could to reach Albany. Clinton was also in need of direction, having heard nothing from Howe since early September and more importantly not knowing the location of Washington's army. In frustration he wrote to Howe on 9 October requesting

---

6   Burgoyne to Clinton, 29 September 1777, quoted in Clinton, *American Rebellion*, p.72.

'what commands you may have for the small corps under my orders, I am at a loss to determine what to do.'[7]

Clinton attempted to send an optimistic note north to Burgoyne on 10 October. While in earlier messages Clinton told Burgoyne that while the way to Albany was open he had insufficient forces available to make the effort in this note Clinton promised to redouble his efforts to reach Albany and supply him with provisions if Burgoyne had decided to continue south. One courier was captured and hanged while the other two found their way barred and returned to Clinton.

With limited resources Clinton could do no more than dismantle Fort Montgomery, improve the defenses at Fort Clinton for a small British garrison, and assign Major General Vaughn to defend Verplanck's Point. While Clinton sought a way to assist Burgoyne he was also well aware that any further movement towards Albany would reduce his ability defend New York. Without information concerning the current location of the American army the possibility of a surprise American attack was always present.

Clinton's anxiety about the safety of New York were improved on receiving a note from Major General Pigot, commander of the Rhode Island garrison, offering to transfer 1,000 men to New York for Clinton's use. With these reinforcements Clinton resolved to reverse course and push up the Hudson towards Albany. He ordered two Hessian regiments and the British 54th Foot up from New York and the transfer of six months provisions for 5,000 men onto boats.

On 13 October, 1777 Clinton directed Vaughn with 2,000 men to move north to make contact with Burgoyne, presumably at Albany, and promised to send additional troops and supplies as necessary. Clinton's hope was that this expedition would create a distraction that would facilitate either Burgoyne's advance to Albany or retreat to Canada. On 15 October Vaughn landed at Kingston, destroying American defensive works and driving off the small detachment of militia. Advancing a further 12 miles north on 17 October to Livingston's Manor, forty-five miles from Albany, the British force discovered that their transports were ill equipped to navigate the shallower waters of this section of the Hudson River. Vaughn reported to Clinton that significant American troops occupied both banks of the Hudson and more importantly he had gathered information, albeit mostly rumors, that Burgoyne had been defeated and was retreating to Canada. It was not until 24 October that Vaughn received the news that Burgoyne had in fact surrendered on 17 October.

With dwindling hope that he could be of assistance to Burgoyne, Clinton's plans to establish a formal presence in the Highlands were dashed when on 17 October he received orders from Howe to detach 4,000 men to reinforce the main army at Philadelphia. Believing Burgoyne was retreating to Canada but lacking any firm information about the status of Burgoyne's army, Clinton had no choice but to recall Vaughn on 22 October and withdraw all his forces to New York. Clinton's first foray into the Highlands had ended in disappointment and embarrassment. He had hoped that Howe would see the strategic advantage Clinton had gained by securing a large

---

7   Quoted in William B. Wilcox, *Portrait of a General* (New York: Knopf, 1962), p.185.

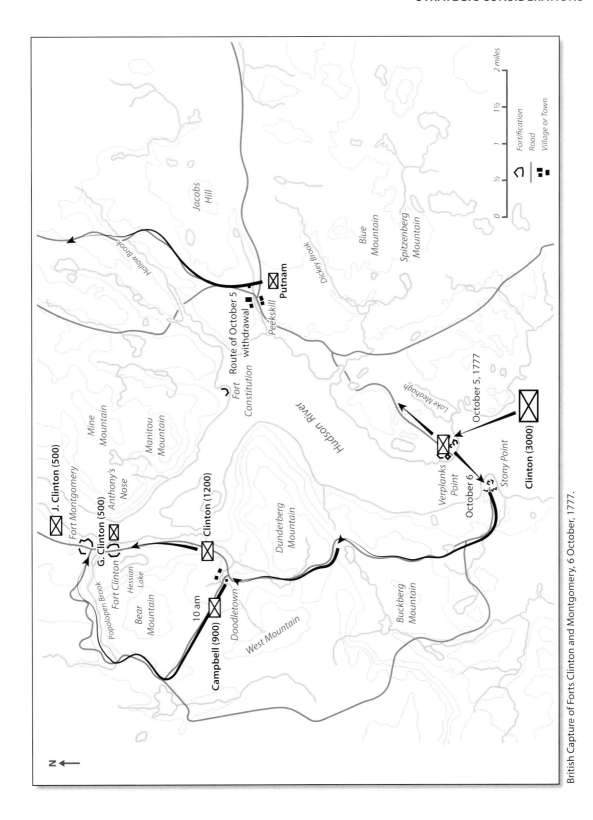

British Capture of Forts Clinton and Montgomery, 6 October, 1777.

portion of the Hudson River, including the capture of the key American forts protecting navigation and the critical link at Kings Ferry, effectively cutting communications between New England and the lower Colonies. Howe's demand for reinforcements effectively ended any hope for securing British gains in the Highlands and Clinton returned to New York bitterly resenting what he believed was a missed opportunity.

In the aftermath of the failed defense of the Highlands, the process to strengthen the fortifications was further frustrated by continuing arguments between engineers and military leadership about the desirability of devoting resources to fortifying West Point or reoccupying the existing string of forts. Discouraged at the continued threat to the Highlands and West Point Washington wrote to Major General Israel Putnam on 2 December 1777. 'The importance of the North River in the present contest and the necessity of defending it, are subjects which have been so frequently and so fully discussed and are so well understood, that it is unnecessary to enlarge upon them.'[8] Washington reminded Putnam that the Highlands held the key to communications and the movement of men and supplies between New England and the remainder of the colonies. He concluded the letter encouraging Putnam to accelerate the strengthening of the defenses and warning him that the British could return in the spring to ravage the countryside.

The disputes over the Hudson defenses continued even after the decision was made to focus efforts on West Point, with disagreements between engineers over the design of the defenses. During the remainder of 1777 and early 1778 the only progress in improving the Hudson River defenses was the deployment of a new chain across the water between West Point and Constitution Island. In April, 1778 Polish-born engineer Thaddeus Kosciuszko was appointed chief engineer at West Point and the defenses began to take shape. By the middle of 1779 the West Point defenses consisted of a set of mutually supporting strongpoints and were the key to maintaining American control over the Hudson Highlands. As part of the chain of fortifications along the Hudson River the Americans built a earthen redoubt, Fort Lafayette, on the east bank at Verplanck's Point and a wooden blockhouse on the west bank at Stony Point.

Clinton naturally understood the importance of the Hudson Highlands and West Point and was certain that Washington could be compelled to respond to a British threat to capture key areas along the Hudson River and, more specifically, a direct attack on West Point. With that in mind Clinton's thoughts turned again to the area around Stony Point and Verplanck's Point which included the strategic Kings Ferry crossing. Clinton's experience in the fall of 1777 along the Hudson was still a fresh memory and he remembered having used Stony Point as a jumping-off place for an offensive against American forts further north. Most recently the significance of Kings Ferry was again demonstrated when the Americans moved the Convention Army, those British troops held captive as a result of Burgoyne's surrender, from New England to Pennsylvania in late 1778. Kings Ferry was used to transfer the captives across the Hudson and although Clinton's attempt to interdict

8   Washington to Putnam, 2 December 1777, *Founders Online,* National Archives.

the movement and rescue the prisoners had fallen short he was once again reminded of the importance of Stony Point and Verplanck's Point.

British intelligence sources, primarily Loyalist spies and American deserters, provided Clinton with tantalizing information about the state of American defenses at Kings Ferry. Clinton knew from these sources that fortifications at both Stony Point and Fort Lafayette were undermanned and he concluded both could be taken without serious opposition. Washington continued to be concerned about the perceived and real weakness of the Highland defenses. Major General Alexander McDougall, in command of American forces in the Highlands, operated an extensive intelligence gathering network and in March 1779 passed along information to Washington that there was some evidence that a British offensive might be in the offing. In response to this information Washington wrote to McDougall on 6 March 1779: 'The bare suggestion of an attempt upon the posts in the Highlands (whether true or false) makes me extremely solicitous to have the Works at Westpoint pushed forward with all possible dispatch.' [9]

Clinton nascent optimism was further buoyed by the success of Commodore George Collier's expedition to raid Virginia. Clinton had ordered the raids, in part to fulfill Germain's directive to undertake strikes at the American supply bases and privateer centers in New England and in Virginia. In little over two weeks Collier's fleet, assisted by Major General Edward Mathew's infantry, had ravaged the Virginia coastline, capturing or destroying large quantities of magazines, gunpowder, and naval stores, including cannon and hogsheads of valuable tobacco. At Portsmouth the British seized supplies and burned ships and then fanned out to ravage Norfolk, Gosport, and Suffolk. Over 130 American naval vessels of various sizes were either captured or destroyed. Collier was encouraged by his success and impressed by the attitude of the Virginia Loyalists, writing to Clinton, 'Our success and the present appearance of things infinitely exceed our most sanguine expectations; and, if the various accounts the General [Matthews] and myself have received can be depended on, the most flattering hopes of return to obedience to their sovereign may be expected from most of this province.' [10] Collier proposed establishing a permanent base at Portsmouth, Virginia that could accommodate his fleet and allow for further incursions into Virginia or the Carolinas.

Clinton referred the matter to Major General Mathew, writing him on 20 May, 1779. Clinton's letter noted the enthusiasm expressed by Collier for establishing a permanent base at Portsmouth and his opinion that conditions seemed ripe for encouraging Virginia Loyalists to rally to the Crown. At the same time Clinton seemed skeptical about the long term Loyalist commitment and reminded Mathew that he had been counting on the return of his forces to allow for future operations in the New York area. In the end Clinton was sanguine enough to leave the decision to Mathew, who decided against establishing the base at Portsmouth. Collier's fleet and Mathew's men returned to New York on 28 May 1779. With Matthew's force

---

9   Washington to McDougall, 6 March 1779, *Founders Online,* National Archives.
10   Quoted in Clinton, *The American Rebellion*, p.406.

returned and Collier's fleet available to quickly and safely ferry his men to Stony Point, Clinton finalized his plans.

Looking forward to the 1779 campaign Clinton adopted a strategy of indirect maneuvers designed to flush Washington out from his Middlebrook bastion before the new state levies could join him to reinforce the Continental Army. By dispatching Collier and Mathew to Virginia, Clinton hoped Washington's attention would also be drawn to the south, allowing Clinton to initiate the second phase of his strategy, a move to capture the Kings Ferry and the forts at Verplank's Point and Stony Point.

Encamped at Middlebrook through the early spring of 1779, Washington kept a close watch on Clinton's movements. Utilizing the extensive espionage network that had been developed since the beginning of the war, Washington received regular reports on British troop movements and other activity that might provide some insight into Clinton's intentions for the upcoming campaign season. Despite the availability of accurate information about British activity the interpretation of that information was usually speculative and most of the time incorrect. On 17 April, 1779 Brigadier General Maxwell, who oversaw the day to day intelligence gathering activities for Washington, reported that a large flotilla of British ships was about to depart New York bound for Rhode Island. Maxwell speculated that this might portend a British evacuation of the Rhode Island garrison. Maxwell reaffirmed his supposition that the British might abandon Rhode Island in a 22 April 1779 dispatch but cautioned that other activity suggested British troops were about to embark on an expedition to either the West Indies or Georgia. He reported that nine regiments with baggage and supplies were being loaded onto the ships.

The next day Washington duly passed along Maxwell's information to Major General McDougall but correctly assessed that the loading of baggage and supplies did not support a possible British attack up the Hudson. Hedging his bets, Washington also forwarded Maxwell's information to Major General Israel Putnam that same day, noting that the real purpose of the British 'commotions' remained a mystery and reaffirmed his anxiety about a possible British thrust into the Highlands. In consequence of his concerns he ordered Putnam to place his command on alert and ready to move into the Highlands no later than 10 May 1779.

Washington continued to receive information and speculation from various sources about British intentions. On 28 April Washington, still uncertain about British plans, wrote Putnam, 'there is great reason to suspect the enemy has some important movement in contemplation'[11] and ordered him to immediately detach one of his two brigades to reinforce Major General McDougall and keep the remaining brigade in readiness to march.

After receiving a dispatch from Maxwell on 3 May, 1779 which included information about the embarkation of four British regiments, but no clue as to their destination, Washington wrote to McDougall expressing frustration that he 'was at a loss how to consider the intelligence' and requesting McDougall collect more detailed information on British activity. Maxwell wrote again on 5 May, reaffirming the information about the four regiments and suggested they were bound for Georgia or the West Indies

---

11   Washington to Putnam, 28 April 1779, *Founders Online*, National Archives.

when in reality they were part of the task force that had been dispatched to raid the Virginia coastline. Washington had more detailed information on the composition of the British expedition on 8 May but was still under the impression the fleet was bound for Georgia. On that date McDougall also provided a detailed description of recent British activity to improve their fortifications around the Kingsbridge area and cautioned Washington that his sources continued to suggest a British movement up the North River. Maxwell finally confirmed on 12 May that approximately 4,000 British troops under the command of Major General Mathew had sailed south to raid the coast from the Chesapeake Bay to Charleston and that reinforcements from England were soon expected to arrive in New York.

With the intelligence that the majority of the British warships were absent from New York Washington proposed to John Jay , President of the Continental Congress, on 17 May, and subsequently to the Continental Congress Marine Committee, that conditions might be favorable for a surprise raid by American frigates to destroy the British transports that remained in the harbor. Samuel Adams replied on behalf of the Committee to Washington on 26 May, rejecting the proposed attack as impractical given the condition of the small American fleet but promising to consider any future projects Washington might propose.

Although recent British activity had been focused on expeditions to the southern colonies Washington continued to be gather strong evidence of their continued interest in the Hudson Highlands. On 17 May Washington received a long message detailing conversations between Elijah Hunter, a double agent, and British officials concerning the strength and disposition of American forces in the Highlands. The British were also very interested in knowing if Washington might respond to a British raid into Connecticut by detaching troops under McDougall's command from the Highlands, weakening the garrisons along the Hudson. The informant was certain that the British were intent on capturing West Point and the posts along the Hudson. He also passed along information that Clinton was expecting a return of the units sent to the West Indies, and reinforcements from England. His information suggested that the capture of Charleston was a major British objective, in order to rally the Loyalists in South Carolina to the Crown and to disrupt the flow of supplies and armaments to the Americans. McDougall wrote to Washington on 23 May relating the details of a similar conversation between one of his agents and British officers. In his note McDougall admitted he had not taken seriously the prospect of a major British attack but was now believed an attack probable.

By 24 May Washington's review of the accumulated information convinced him that Clinton was planning an attack, either on the main American army or an advance up the Hudson and as a consequence alerted Major General Israel Putnam that the British were assembling and repairing a fleet of flat bottom boats for the operation. He reminded Putnam that he should be prepared to march from his base at Redding, Connecticut along with Brigadier General Parson's brigade as soon as information on a British advance was received. As anxiety grew over the imminent British attack Major General McDougall repositioned Brigadier General Nixon's and

Patterson's brigades to cover enemy landings on either bank of the Hudson and suggested that Putnam and Parson's brigade be moved closer to the Highlands from Redding.

On 28 May Washington issued a circular to his senior generals summarizing the information gathered about British resources and intentions. In it Washington declared that British strength at New York was approximately 9,000 while the British garrison at Rhode Island numbered somewhere between 5,000 and 6,000. The remainder of British troops were deployed in Georgia and Virginia. While noting there could be no absolute certainty about British plans Washington declared that Clinton seemed set to deploy approximately 5,000 men for operations in the Hudson Highlands.

The circular also identified the current disposition of American forces. The Maryland, Pennsylvania and Virginia troops were deployed at Middlebrook and North Carolina troops at Paramus, New Jersey. Three Massachusetts and one Connecticut brigade were positioned to defend the Highlands along the North River, while another Connecticut brigade was located at Danbury, Connecticut and approximately 2,500 men were at Rhode Island. These forces were within two to three days march from assembling to defend West Point. The remaining American troops were expected to be used in the offensive against the Indians along the western frontier. After subtracting sick, absent or otherwise unavailable Washington estimated his available strength at 11,800. Washington closed the circular with a pessimistic assessment of potential reinforcements and a request that officers provide him with their thoughts on how best to utilize the available forces.

In response to his request for suggestions for the coming campaign Washington received varying levels of support for an attack on New York, based on overly optimistic assessments of American strength and capabilities. Aware of the suggestions being given Washington, Major General Nathanael Greene prepared a lengthy and sober reflection on the possibilities of attacking New York. After describing the disposition of British troops and possible responses to an attack on New York, Greene noted that while he ardently wished an attempt on New York could be attempted he did not believe it would be successful. He reminded Washington that 'the great object of the Enemies attention is and ever ought to have been our Army-destroy that and the Country is conquer'd; or at least this is the most ready way to affect a reduction of the United States.'[12]

Washington received news on 30 May from Colonel De Hart from Bergen, New Jersey that the bulk of British troops in New York had marched to Kingsbridge and their fleet of boats had been sent up the North River. Additional intelligence was provided by New Jersey militia Colonel John Neilson, who reported that British deserters had confirmed a force estimated at 8,000 had been collected at White Plains.

The information from Neilson presaged Clinton's long awaited movement up the Hudson. When Collier's fleet returned to New York on 28 May, Clinton had already ordered Major General John Vaughn to advance north from Kingsbridge to Phillipsburg with a mixed force that included British regulars, light infantry, and grenadiers, as well as Hessian regiments,

---

12 Greene to Washington, 31 May 1779, *Founders Online*, National Archives.

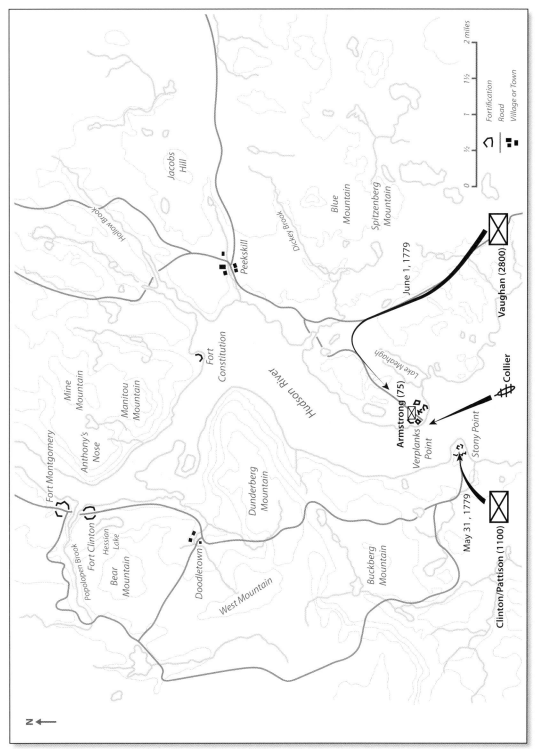

British Capture of Kings Crossing, 31 May, 1779.

Loyalist infantry, and cavalry. The British moved north in four columns and established camp on Valentine's Hill, near Phillipsburg. Two British and three Hessian regiments were left to defend the lines at Kingsbridge while two British Guards battalions and three Hessian regiments remained in New York. Additional British and Loyalist regiments defended Staten Island.

Collier's fleet, with Mathew's men still aboard, was joined by the warships *Camilla* and *Raisonable* and sailed north to join Vaughn at Phillipsburg. On 30 May Clinton joined Collier on the *Camilla*. Clinton's plan for the capture of the Kings Ferry included three separate commands. Major General James Pattison, with the 17th, 63rd and 64th Foot, along with a detachment of Hessian *Jaegers*, was assigned to land south of the Stony Point position and move quickly to capture the American blockhouse and secure the western shore.

Major General Vaughn was assigned a mixed force of 2,800 men, composed of British light infantry, grenadiers, the 33rd Foot, Hessian grenadiers, and Loyalist troops from the British Legion, Loyal American Regiment, and Ferguson's rifle corps. Vaughn's men were to land on the east bank at Tellers Point, and then march eight miles north to invest Fort Lafayette at Verplanck's Point. Collier's ships sailed north to support both attacks from the river.

At 4.00 pm on 31 May Pattison landed the 17th, 63rd, and 64th Foot along with 120 Hessian *Jaegers*, under the direct command of Lieutenant Colonel Henry Johnson. Accompanied by Clinton, Lieutenant Colonel Johnson advanced against the American blockhouse at Stony Point. At the appearance of the British column, the American defenders set fire to the blockhouse and retreated. Immediately on Johnson's men securing the Stony Point position, Pattison landed four cannon and three mortars and spent the night manhandling the guns to the summit. Taking advantage of the moonlight Pattison utilized 58 soldiers in harnesses and others pushing the guns up the steep slope, and by dawn had established two batteries overlooking Fort Lafayette. Prior to occupying Stony Point the British had estimated the distance across the Hudson to Fort Lafayette to be 800 to 900 yards. Once positioned on the summit they quickly realized the actual distance was closer to 1,500 yards rendering several of the light artillery pieces ineffective. The remaining guns began a steady bombardment that destroyed one American gun and killed three defenders.

On the opposite shore Major General Vaughn landed his force eight miles south of Verplanck's Point on the morning of 31 May and moved north. At daybreak on 1 June, Vaughn's men methodically surrounded the American defenses at Fort Lafayette while the newly-established batteries on Stony Point, supported by the guns of the *Camilla* and several other smaller galleys and gunboats, opened fire on the American position.

Fort Lafayette was defended by 70 men of the 5th North Carolina Regiment, commanded by Captain Thomas Armstrong. The fort's defenses included a wooden palisade located behind earthen parapets, protected by a ditch. The fort also included a wooden blockhouse and a barbette battery consisting of one 18lb and two 4lb guns, facing the Hudson. By midday Armstrong recognized the impossibility of his situation, surrounded and outnumbered and subjected to constant artillery fire from Stony Point, and entered into a brief negotiation with Vaughn before surrendering the fort by midday.

Under the direction of British engineers, work began immediately to improve the Stony Point fortifications. Firing platforms were constructed and the surrounding woods were cleared to create more effective fields of fire. The trees were then used to create abatis by sharpening the branches and laying the trees side by side, sharpened branches pointed towards the direction of enemy approach, intertwining the branches where possible, and staking the trees to the ground to create a stable, continuous barrier.

Clinton, accompanied by half his forces, returned to Phillipsburg on 4 June, watching closely to see how Washington would react to the loss of the Kingsbridge crossing.

On 31 May Washington received a hurriedly composed message from McDougall, written the evening of 30 May, reporting 40 or more British vessels embarking troops for movement up the North River. On the morning of 1 June McDougall prepared a more detailed description of the British offensive. He reported that the previous day the British force, which included units recently returned from the Virginia expedition, had sailed to Haverstraw Bay, just south of Kings Ferry, and disembarked. McDougall ordered the blockhouse on the west bank at Stony Point abandoned and burned. He observed that the British seemed reluctant to proceed past American fortifications on the east bank at Verplanck's Point. McDougall ordered the North Carolina brigade to fall back to West Point, supplies to be removed from Fishkill, and militia called out to meet the British threat.

With McDougall's report in hand, Washington immediately alerted his general staff to the British advance and ordered them to be ready to move. He also cancelled the court-martial of Brigadier General Benedict Arnold, scheduled to begin that day to consider charges leveled at Arnold by Philadelphia officials during his tenure as commander of the Philadelphia garrison.

On 2 June Washington alerted McDougall that New York militia reported the British force included both transports and flat bottomed boats capable of navigating the Hudson River. In a reference to the feints Clinton used during the 1777 campaign to confuse Putnam, resulting in Putnam dispersing his forces and allowing Clinton to capture Forts Montgomery and Clinton, Washington wrote 'I doubt not you will keep your force collected and your attention fixed on the forts, notwithstanding all the demonstrations the enemy will make, which will naturally wear a variety of faces.'[13] Orders were also issued to the divisions of the army directing them to positions intended to respond to the British threat.

Describing the British advance up the Hudson as a 'crisis' Washington notified his staff that he expected to leave Middlebrook on 3 June bound for Smith's Clove where he could better monitor the evolving situation. He also kept key members of the Continental Congress informed about the British offensive. Smith's Clove was a valley approximately 15 miles west of the Hudson River, running parallel for approximately 23 miles from northern

---

13 Washington to McDougall, 2 June 1779, Founders Online, National Archives.

The British were aware of Washington's redeployment into the Clove. Writing on 9 June, to Lord Townsend, Major General Pattison noted that deserters had confirmed Washington had marched his army from New Jersey to the Clove. Pattison estimated Washington's force totaled approximately 6,000 and that Washington was not certain whether to march to West Point or back to Middlebrook. Pattison also included in his note a sketch of the West Point defenses, prepared from information from another deserter. The deserter had also confirmed the West Point forts were defended by seven New England regiments and two from North Carolina.

After several days waiting for the British to make their next move Washington wrote to New York Governor George Clinton requesting he dismiss the militia rather than keep them under arms but inactive. During this time he received reports that the British were improving the position at Verplanck's Point and expanding the fortifications at Stony Point while also returning a portion of the British forces to New York. On 11 June McDougall wrote to Washington expressing frustration that he would be unable to protect the stores of supplies along the east bank with his available forces if the British advanced in strength. He also noted that various British deserters were in agreement that the works at West Point were the ultimate goal of the British offensive.

Accordingly, on 12 June Washington issued orders that the Virginia, Maryland, and Pennsylvania divisions were to create companies of light infantry composed of men from each regiment whom the commanding officer believed would 'support the reputation of his regiment.' Contingency orders were also issued outlining the general dispositions of the Army in case of an attack on West Point. The divisions deployed in the Clove were directed to concentrate at the Furnace of Dean, a foundry located 6 miles northwest of Fort Montgomery. The next day Washington, as he had done in the past, requested his senior commanders provide him with their thinking about possible British intentions and recommendations on how the army might react in the event of a British attack on West Point. With these arrangements made Washington issued an order to all senior commanders reminding them of the need to vigorously resist any British attack on West Point and designated Major General Israel Putnam to assume temporary command of the army while he traveled to West Point on 15 June.

As Washington rode to West Point he was cautiously optimistic. Although initially surprised by Clinton's attack on the Kings Ferry and disappointed by the loss of Fort Lafayette and Stony Point he had be able to respond with some alacrity, moving the bulk of his army into a position to respond to Clinton's next move. Clinton's lethargy after the bold push up the Hudson to Kings Ferry still perplexed him. Although he still viewed control of the Hudson Highlands and possession of West Point as essential to the viability of the American war effort, he continued to be wary of overreacting and placing the Continental Army at risk of a general engagement with the British on unequal terms.

On 21 June Washington issued orders moving his headquarters to New Windsor, New York and assigned Major General Israel Putnam command of the Continental forces aligned along Smith's Clove. New Windsor was a small village, located along the Hudson River, 13 miles north of West Point. Washington chose to relocate his headquarters to New Windsor to have more ready access to West Point, reemphasizing the importance of that place. On the same day Washington received a detailed intelligence report from Major Henry Lee, Jr. whose mixed force of cavalry and infantry had been shadowing British forces around Stony Point. Lee reported information gleaned from several British deserters, which confirmed that two British regiments, the 63rd and 64th Foot, along with wounded, women and children, and their associated baggage were being withdrawn from Stony Point. Lee noted that Clinton had not yet returned from New York and that Lieutenant Colonel Henry Johnson of the 17th Foot was in command of Stony Point. Lee's intelligence also included a summary of the British naval forces operating at the Kings Ferry and a detailed description of the British fortifications and artillery at Stony Point. Lee included his assessment that Clinton's intention was to initiate operations along the East River, leaving a small garrison to guard the Kings Crossing forts. Washington immediately forwarded Lee's intelligence to Major General McDougall, commander at West Point, suggesting some sort of British movement was imminent. Two days later Washington's staff alerted Putnam that a strong force of British infantry had been spotted on the east bank of the Hudson near Fort Montgomery and he should be prepared to respond as necessary. British intentions were still anything but clear.

4

Pause

Just as Washington felt unease at his future prospects, Clinton believed his capture of Kings Ferry would achieve his overall objective of forcing Washington to leave the Middlebrook encampment. An army on the march offers many more opportunities for fatal missteps, the delay or loss of orders to one or more elements, misinterpretation of orders, weather related delays in movement; all create situations in which an enemy can interpose his forces and attack his opponent piecemeal or in an unfavorable disposition. Although Clinton was aware of the movements of the Continental Army along the Smith's Clove position he was unwilling to attempt to interdict Washington's vulnerable forces due to lingering concerns about the safety of New York City. Clinton had missed an opportunity to capture West Point. Washington had realistically concluded that with the quick capture of Fort Lafayette and Stony Point Clinton could have pushed rapidly north and seriously threatened the West Point position. The concerns that kept Clinton from exploiting his initial success at Kings Ferry now kept him from taking another bold step.

Clinton could have attacked Washington's army as it redeployed along the Smith's Clove Road but lingering concerns about the weakness of the garrison left at New York haunted him., Despite concluding that a strike at the Continentals at Smith's Clove was too risky Clinton believed that Washington's repositioned army would be unable to survive with supplies from the surrounding area and would be largely dependent on their bases at Trenton and Germantown. Sensing a new opportunity Clinton plotted a movement into New Jersey, intended to cut off the Americans from their source of supplies, with the expectation that Washington would then be forced to respond to the British movement. Clinton ultimately decided against this strategy, again due to the concern that moving the bulk of his army away from New York could endanger the remaining garrison. Clinton briefly considered a scaled-back effort involving only the use of his cavalry to raid the American supply depots and artillery parks. More prudent officers convinced Clinton to abandon the idea.Clinton took some solace from his occupation of Kings Ferry, cutting off a key communications link between New England and the Middle Colonies and adding an additional 90 miles to the movement of Washington's supplies.

Clinton's main concerns in developing the next phase of the campaign was his lack of adequate resources and uncertainty over when the promised reinforcements from England would arrive or the West Indies expedition would return. Clinton had been promised an additional 6,000 men from England and expected the return of a portion of Grant's West Indies expedition. He had calculated, wrongly as it turned out, that the British fleet would set sail in April and arrive in New York in late May or early June. Rather than sailing as scheduled in April, contrary winds delayed Vice Admiral Arbuthnot's fleet for a month. The French attack on the island of Jersey further delayed Arbuthnot, resulting in another delay. The fleet did not sail until 4 June, about the time Clinton had expected the fleet to arrive.

Now, with no clear idea when the additional troops might arrive, Clinton had to decide what he could do with his limited resources. The standoff continued into the middle of June as Clinton and Washington eyed each other warily. Clinton still retained the initiative but the campaign season was well advanced and without the additional forces from England he did not believe he could initiate a direct campaign against either Washington's army or the West Point forts.

Clinton actions and ultimate objectives were never completely clear with his own subordinates.. Clinton's lunge north to capture Stony Point and Verplank's Point was either the precursor to a broader British offensive to capture West Point or a limited attack intended to lure Washington into a decisive battle to protect his lines of communication to New England. Clinton's 1777 success in capturing Forts Montgomery and Clinton inclined him to continue to push north but without additional forces he did not believe he was strong enough to invest West Point and protect New York. With no clear idea of when the additional forces might arrive, and given Washington's reticence to be drawn into battle, Clinton had to find another option.

While Washington's main concern was the safety and protection of West Point the British occupation of the Kings Ferry created logistical problems that would have to be addressed.

Recognizing Washington's continuing difficulties in supplying his army Clinton concluded that a more direct threat to the source of those supplies might induce Washington to react. With the success of the recent Chesapeake raid Clinton prepared a plan to send an expedition into Connecticut to capture supplies and disrupt the centers of privateer activity that continued to prey on British shipping.

On 1 July a combined land and naval force of 5,000 men, many drawn from the Rhode Island garrison, under the overall command of New York Governor Major General William Tryon, boarded ships in New York with the objective of attacking New Haven. New Haven had long been a center of American privateering and Clinton's orders to Tyron were very specific. Clinton proposed that Tyron begin his raid at New Haven, where Clinton believed several privateers were docked. Clinton's directive to Tyron included specific information about the Continental defenses provided by Loyalist sources. Clinton alerted Tyron to militia defenses located on bluffs that dominated the harbor and cautioned him to remain no more than 48 hours before moving on to Fairfield. Clinton declared that he expected Tyron's raid would force Washington to 'either pass the North river with his whole army or strong detachment, and I wish you to be always within 24 or 48 hours of joining me'.[1]

While the movements of the British 53-vessel fleet, commanded by Commodore Collier, were delayed by unfavorable winds until 3 July, their movements were monitored by American militia soon after leaving New York but their destination was uncertain. Militia in New Haven observed elements of the fleet moving east along the horizon during the afternoon of the 4 July but assumed it was headed for a more distant destination. The fleet began arriving at New Haven late on the evening of 4 July, 1779, was fully assembled by midnight and began disembarking the next morning at 5.00 am The British forces were divided into two divisions. The first division, 1,500 men under the command of Brigadier General George Garth, landed under the protection of the naval guns, without opposition, and marched to West Haven Green. Garth's column was composed of the 23rd and 54th Foot, the light infantry companies of the British Guards, and the Hessian *Jaegers*, supported by four field guns manned by the Royal Artillery.

The second division also totaled approximately 1,500 men and was led by Major General Tryon. Tryon's force, including the 23rd Foot, the Hessian Landgrave Regiment, and the King's American Regiment along with a two gun battery, began landing at 8.00 pm and was opposed by a small force of New Haven militia. The militia, numbering little more than 50, deployed cannon at Morris Point to oppose the British landing. Fire from the cannon caused Tyron's forces to split into two groups. Small parties of militia briefly resisted both groups. Militia fire killed a Loyalist officer and in response, upon landing, several houses and barns were burned.

After forming on the beach and deploying skirmishers to protect their flanks Tyron's force moved inland, pushing aside the militia forces that attempted to disrupt in their advanceThroughout the day militia strength continued to increase as small bands from outlying towns made their way towards New Haven. During their pursuit of militia units, Tyron's force also burned homes and farms and devastated the area. Tryon's force pushed forward to occupy a portion of East Haven while Tyron made his headquarters at Beacon Hill. That evening Tryon held a council with Commodore Collier and Brigadier General Garth in the Old State House. The council members noted the unexpectedly strong resistance of the local militia and decided to re-embark the next day when the tide allowed the fleet to move. It was agreed that Garth's force would occupy New Haven while Tyron's column would defend Beacon Hill.

The next morning the British set fire to buildings and ships at the wharf and aided by a dense fog re-embarked. By late afternoon on 6 July the last British ships slipped out of the harbor. Tyron had suffered more than 100 dead and wounded and left behind 27 houses and another 20 buildings destroyed and seven ships burned.

---

1   'Instructions to Maj. Gen. Tryon,' Charles Hervey Townshend, *The British Invasion of New Haven, Connecticut, Together with Some Account of Their Landing and Burning of the Towns of Fairfield and Norwalk, July 1779* (New Haven, Ct., 1879), p.33.

Light infantry from various regiments were drawn together to form the Continental attack columns. Each wore their own distinctive regimental uniform in a variety of colors, facings and headgear. The left and center figures represent Pennsylvania and Connecticut privates respectively, while the figure on the right is an officer from North Carolina. The officer carries a spontoon, issued by order of George Washington to all the officers in the Stony Point assault. (Original artwork by Ed Dovey © Helion & Company)

The main force of British defenders at Stony Point were from the 17th Foot, shown on the right. Also composing the Stony Point garrison were men from the Loyal American Regiment, center, and grenadiers from the 71st Highland Regiment, left. (Original artwork by Ed Dovey © Helion & Company)

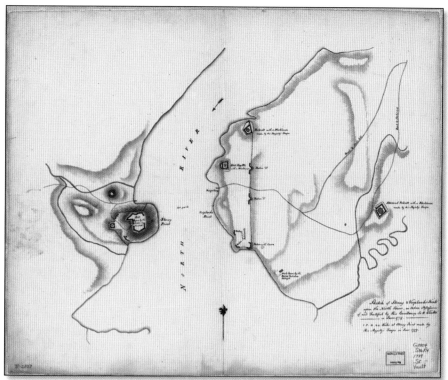

Sketch of Stoney & Verplank's Points upon the North River, as taken possession of, and fortified by His Excellency Sir H: Clinton in June 1779' (Library of Congress).

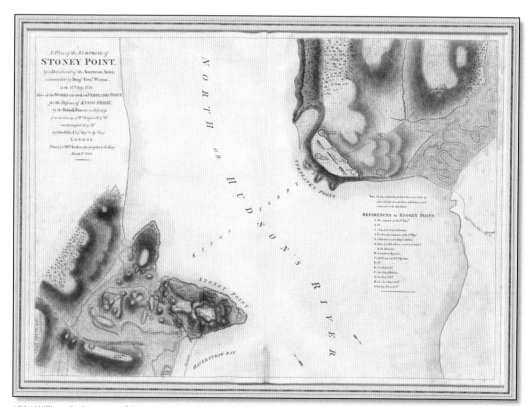

1784 William Faden map of Stony Point and Verplanks Point showing American Assault (Library of Congress).

The assault on the Upper Works. The main assault Continental assault column, commanded by Colonel Christian Febiger, and accompanied by Brigadier General Anthony Wayne, ascended the southern slope of Stony Point, avoiding the Lower Works a▶

broke through the abatis protecting the Upper Works. The illustration shows the Continental light infantry surging over the r Works parapets, defended by men of the British 17th Foot. (Original artwork by Ed Dovey © Helion & Company)

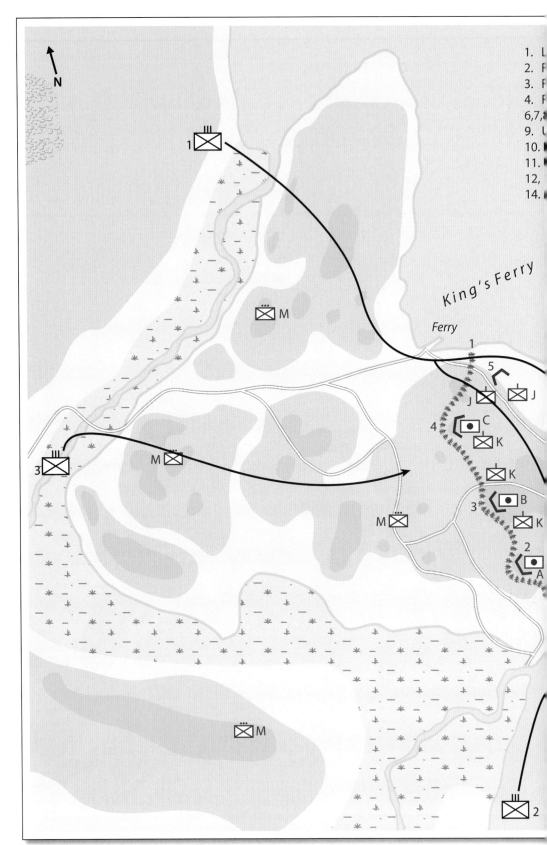

The American assault on Stony Point, 15 July 1779.

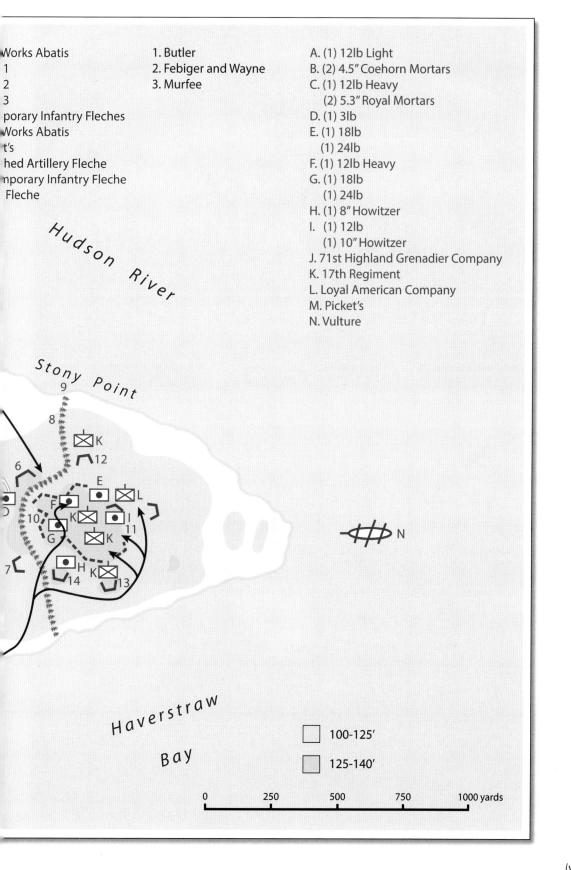

Works Abatis
1
2
3
porary Infantry Fleches
Works Abatis
t's
hed Artillery Fleche
mporary Infantry Fleche
Fleche

1. Butler
2. Febiger and Wayne
3. Murfee

A. (1) 12lb Light
B. (2) 4.5" Coehorn Mortars
C. (1) 12lb Heavy
   (2) 5.3" Royal Mortars
D. (1) 3lb
E. (1) 18lb
   (1) 24lb
F. (1) 12lb Heavy
G. (1) 18lb
   (1) 24lb
H. (1) 8" Howitzer
I. (1) 12lb
   (1) 10" Howitzer
J. 71st Highland Grenadier Company
K. 17th Regiment
L. Loyal American Company
M. Picket's
N. Vulture

Hudson River

Stony Point

Haverstraw

Bay

100-125'

125-140'

0   250   500   750   1000 yards

Battle of Stony Point fresco in US Capitol Rotunda, showing a wounded Anthony Wayne carried into the fortifications (Library of Congress).

Looking east across the Hudson River to Verplank's Point, located in the area of the white house (Author's photo).

Collier's fleet sailed 25 miles west, along the Long Island Sound, towards Fairfield. In addition to being a prosperous farming community the port served several privateers and a flour mill and gunpowder mill were a source of supplies for the Continental army. Just as at New Haven local militia observed the British ships early morning 7 July but assumed they were returning to New York. A heavy fog blanketed the coast later in the morning and at 10.00 am when the fog cleared the local militia were stunned to find the British fleet at anchor several miles offshore. At 4.00 pm. Tyron landed a force composed of the Guards light companies, Hessian Landgrave Regiment, King's American Regiment, and two guns approximately one and one-half miles from Fairfield, near Black Rock Fort. Tyron's column marched to Fairfield with swarms of militia hanging on their flanks, trying unsuccessfully to slow their advance. Despite the militia opposition Tyron occupied Fairfield and was soon joined by Garth's forces which landed around noon. After several hours of ravaging the town, under cover of a thunderstorm, Tyron's forces retired at 8.00 pm and re-embarked early the next morning. The damage to Fairfield was much more severe than that suffered by New Haven. Over 200 buildings, homes, and barns were burned.

Tyron sailed to Huntington, Long Island and spent the next several days gathering supplies and resting his men. On the afternoon of 11 July his fleet once again appeared off the coast of Connecticut, near Norwalk. Like New Haven and Fairfield Norwalk was home to several privateers and a major supply source for the Continental Army. At nightfall Tryon landed without opposition and marched early the next morning, 12 July towards Norwalk. While Tryon's force began its march Garth's troops began landing and before noon the combined British force entered Norwalk. Although the Americans were able to assemble of force of about 800 militia buttressed by 150 Continentals they were unable to disrupt the British advance. Just as at New Haven and Fairfield the British and Hessian troops desolated the town, burning over 200 homes, barns and shops. Mills and ships were also destroyed before Tyron's men marched back to the beach at nightfall.

While Tyron's men were terrorizing the Connecticut countryside, Clinton kept a cautious watch on Washington's actions and looked expectantly for the long promised reinforcements. Just as Washington had received a constant stream of intelligence on British movements and dispositions, Clinton also benefited from information from deserters and Loyalists. From these various sources Clinton had a reasonable estimate of Washington's overall strength and knew that Continental troops were deployed on both banks of the Hudson and in Smith's Clove. In order to support Tyron's raids and be in position to respond to the hoped for movement of Washington's army into Connecticut Clinton shifted his forces eastward along the Long Island Sound to Byram and Mamoroneck.

For his part Washington continued to believe that Clinton's main objectives were the capture of West Point and the defeat the Continental Army if it attempted to come to the assistance of the forts. On 1 July, as Tryon was sailing from New York towards his first target at New Haven, Washington prepared his thoughts on the defense of West Point. Washington correctly identified Clinton's options, noting that the British were either intent on capturing West Point, forcing the American army to battle, or both. In the document Washington laid out several scenarios, postulating about British movements along either the east or west banks of the Hudson River. After enumerating the British options as he saw them Washington raised the question of 'what is the proper line of conduct for us to observe' and concluded by proposing they use 'every possible means to discover the real design of the enemy, & distinguish feints from serious movements'.[2]

---

2   'Thoughts on Defense of West Point, July 1779' *Founders Online*, National Achieves.

5

The Gibraltar of America

Clinton's dilemma was an all too obvious lack of resources necessary to carry out his multi- faceted strategy. Although he had enough troops at hand to capture the Kings Ferry defenses of Stony Point and Verplank's Point, he hesitated to either continue on to attack West Point or threaten Washington's supply centers in New Jersey due to nagging misgivings that he could not undertake either action and continue to ensure the protection of his base at New York City. He eagerly awaited the promised reinforcements from England and the expected return of a portion of the troops he had dispatched to the West Indies. As June turned into July Clinton realized the window was quickly closing on the campaign season and he might not be able to expect any additional resources. Clinton expressed his frustration in a letter to Willian Eden, one of the Peace Commissioners that Clinton had inherited when he took overall command from Howe in 1778, writing 'July and no reinforcements arrived; inadequate as it may be, such as it ought to have been here the first week in June at the furthest.' In the same letter Clinton admitted 'I was lucky in my attempt at Stony Point ... every day proves more, and more its importance.' He then returned to the issue of the promised reinforcements and what he considered a missed opportunity, lamenting that 'had the reenforcements arrived in time to have enabled me to follow it up a general action would have been the consequence; as it is I despair of that'.[1]

In early July, Clinton was forced to transfer troops from the Rhode Island garrison to bolster Tyron's forces for the raids on Connecticut. In order to support Tyron's incursion into Connecticut, and guard against the possibility that Washington might respond by marching to aid Connecticut, Clinton also withdrew troops from the Kings Ferry defenses. He did so 'not entertaining the smallest apprehension that any attempt the enemy could make against that place [Verplank's] or Stony Point could possibly be attended with mischief before I should be able to afford them assistance'. Clinton considered Stony Point the stronger of the two positions, situated on a dominating hilltop and while he did recommend enhanced defenses to guard against a surprise attack he 'looked on the place as perfectly secure with the works already

---

1   Quoted in Henry P. Johnson, *The Storming of Stony Point on the Hudson* (New York: White and Company, 1900), pp.121-122.

Swamp forming the base of the Stony Point position. Continental forces crossed this watercourse in their approach to the British positions (Author's photo).

there, especially as it was under the charge of a vigilant, active and spirited officer and a very amply garrison'.[2]

The Stony Point position was a natural strongpoint, located on the west bank of the Hudson River, across from Verplanck's Point. Located 35 miles north of New York City and 12 miles south of West Point, the summit jutted out into the Hudson River from the west bank, rising 140 feet above the River. The rocky promontory had at its base a marsh which separated it from the mainland. The marsh formed a continuous buffer along the entire western boundary of the rocky outcropping and a small stream, only navigable by small boat during high tide, meandered from north to south. A causeway split the marsh halfway between the north and south shores of the Hudson River. At the summit there was an unobstructed view north to Peekskill Bay and south to Haverstraw Bay. A small cove on the north bank of Stony Point served as the western ferry terminus. Rocky outcroppings dominated the approaches to the summit, restricting access to well-worn paths. Coupled with Verplank's Point on the eastern shore, the two forts constituted the King Ferry which provided essential communications between New England and the middle Colonies.

In order to navigate the bend in the Hudson at King's Crossing ships were required to reduce their speed, making them targets for the artillery on deployed at Verplanck's Point and Stony Point. British Major General Pattison, who participated in its capture and subsequent strengthening, wrote 'Stony Point is by Nature exceedingly strong, from the several Commanding Heights, and being almost insular, by means of a Swamp & Creek from the River, is very inaccessible'[3]

Immediately upon occupying Stony Point the British undertook an extensive program to improve on the Point's natural defenses. Initially overseen by Royal Engineer Captain Alexander Mercer, the woods were cleared from the slopes, improving the fields of fire from the heights against any attackers struggling up towards the defenses. The trees were then used to create abatis, to slow or stop an enemy advance and channel their movement through areas that were prepared to resist an attack.

Two parallel lines of abatis were constructed across the peninsula from the northern to southern shores of the Hudson River. The topography of the

2   Quoted in Clinton, *The American Rebellion*, p.132.
3   Quoted in Johnson, *Storming of Stony Point*, p.118.

summit included a large area of level terrain, referred to by the defenders as the table of the hill. In this area the Upper or Inner Works were constructed. These Upper Works were protected at their base by one line of the abatis. Below the Upper Works the Lower Works were dominated by the rocky outcroppings extending down to the marsh. At the base of the Lower Works the second line the abatis extended across its entire length.

Reconstructed example of temporary fortification used by British to supplement the abatis (Author's photo).

On three outcroppings along the Lower Works the British constructed small forts, referred to as fleches, using a compacted earthen walls reinforced by fascines – large tree limbs bundled together and secured to the sides of the fleches with packed earth. The forts conformed to the shapes of the hill on which they were constructed but generally featured a three sided crescent design, with a front wall through which the cannon were deployed and angled walls on either side. The thickness of the walls ranged from 12 feet at their base to 8 feet at the top. Although the fleches provided the defenders with protection to the front and sides they were open in the rear, which represented a serious weakness. The fleches, numbered One, Two and Three, all faced west towards the marsh. The southernmost fleche, Number One, included a 12lb brass cannon, intended to defend the causeway in case of attack. During daytime six artillerists manned the position, but their numbers were doubled at night. The middle fleche, Number Two was garrisoned by six artillerists armed with a mortar. The northernmost fleche, Number Three also featured a mortar and a 15-man daytime contingent that also doubled at night. Deployed without fortifications behind the lower abatis was a 3lb cannon.

Between the Upper and Lower Works were constructed at least three temporary infantry fleches, made of fence rails formed into a V. These infantry fleches were intended to offer a force of up to 30 men an enhanced level of protection against musket fire. They were positioned to strengthen areas deemed vulnerable, particularly on both flanks.

The Upper Works were also protected by a continuous abatis running along the base of the hilltop table. Although intended to extend the entire length of the hilltop table the abatis was thinnest along the north section and was supplemented by the use of chevaux-de-frise. The chevaux-de-frise consisted of a large center log through which smaller sharpened sticks were imbedded to form a barrier. The chevaux-de-frise were movable and could

Captured three-inch mortar deployed by the British at Stony Point (Author's photo).

be redeployed as necessary to address short term defensive needs.

Within the Upper Works, behind the abatis, around the flatter table the British constructed an earthen parapet, which protected the artillery deployed near the flagpole. This parapet was not continuous and like the fleches included unprotected openings that made them vulnerable to flanking or rear attack. Along sections of the parapet narrow openings, embrasures were provided which allowed cannon to fire through the parapet, towards the enemy. British engineers estimated that the abatis protecting the Upper Works could accommodate 500 men in a single rank, while an additional 300 men could be deployed behind the parapet.

At the southern end of the parapet two cannon, an 18lb and 24lb gun, were deployed to defend the hillside down to the Hudson River waterline. In the middle, near the flagpole, a 12lb cannon was positioned on a platform which allowed the gun to be turned to fire in any direction, while at the northern end an 18lb and 24lb gun covered the northern access up the hill from the Lower Works. While the main defenses were constructed on the table of the Upper Works, the abatis extended further down both hillsides towards the Hudson River. The 18lb and 24lb guns at the northern and southern strongpoints were naval cannon, mounted on truck carriages and then emplaced on firing platforms, restricting their fields of fire. The British knew the northern battery could only adequately cover approximately one half of the hill it was intended to defend.

In addition to the cannon deployed in fixed defenses in the Upper Works, an 8lb howitzer, manned at all times, was deployed and sighted to respond to attackers trying to break through the outer abatis. A 12lb cannon and a 10-inch mortar were positioned near the center of the upper table, oriented towards Verplank's Point. These guns were intended to be emplaced as part of new battery recommended by Captain Mercer. This new battery would also close a gap in the rear defenses of the Upper Works, but at the time of the attack work on the battery had only just begun.

In addition to the cannon deployed within the fortifications the Royal Navy sloop *Vulture* was stationed on the north side of Stony Point. The *Vulture* could support the land defenses with fourteen 6lb cannon. On the south side the row-galley *Cornwallis* could bring fire from one 24lb and four 4lb guns to bear in defense of the lower abatis near the Hudson River. The *Cornwallis* was typically anchored approximately 150 yards from shore, in line with the Upper Works abatis.

The nature of the Stony Point terrain and design of the fortifications put a premium on the special characteristics of mortars to supplement the regular field cannon. Unlike the cannon, whose effective fields of fire were restricted by elevation and intervening obstructions, the mortars fired their ordinance at a high angle, avoiding obstructing terrain and folds in the ground. Rather than using an iron ball to mow down enemy troops, the mortars fired a fused explosive shell that was intended to explode as it neared the ground or after landing. The efficient use of

Recreation of firing platforms used by British for their artillery (Author's photo).

mortars required highly skilled artillerists, able to judge the correct angle of fire and prepare the fuse for the proper timing. Howitzers fulfilled the same role, firing a high trajectory shell designed to drop into fortified positions.

Since his capture of Stony Point and Verplanck's Point in early June Clinton had systematically withdrawn troops from both forts to bolster his efforts elsewhere. On 15 July the garrison of Stony Point was composed of a mixed force of British infantry, Loyalists and artillery, commanded by Lieutenant Colonel Henry Johnson. Eight companies of the Johnson's own 17th Foot, totaling 380 men, made up the bulk of the defenders. The 17th saw service during the 1776 campaign around New York. At the Battle of Princeton the 17th, marching to reinforce British forces pursuing Washington's army after the Christmas attack at Trenton, was surprised, overwhelmed and scattered, the survivors forcing their way through the American lines in a desperate bayonet charge. Reorganized in early 1777, the regiment fought in the 1777 Brandywine and 1778 Monmouth campaigns.

Henry Johnson had served in the West Indies with the 28th Foot during the French and Indian War and accompanied the regiment to America in 1776. Promoted to major, Johnson commanded a provisional light infantry battalion in the 1777 and 1778 campaigns where he was wounded. He was promoted to lieutenant colonel and given command of the 17th in October, 1778.

Also assigned to the Stony Point defense were two companies of grenadiers from the 71st Regiment. Known as Fraser's Highlanders, the 71st had been recruited in Scotland by Major General Simon Fraser. While the bulk of the regiment had been sent to South Carolina in December, 1778 the two grenadier companies, totaling 158 men, had remained with Clinton in New York. The grenadier companies were commanded by Captain Laurence Robert Campbell.

In addition to British regulars the garrison also included 68 men from the Loyal American Regiment. The regiment, recruited from Loyalists from

had overseen the initial preparation of the Stony Point defenses after its capture by the British in early June, 1779. In discussing the Lower Works Mercer testified that the 'intention of these Fleches were for Piquets by day, and a Chain of Sentries by Night'. Mercer thought the 12lb cannon and the two 24lb and 18lb guns deployed in the Upper Works could be used to fire at the fleches of the Lower Works to dislodge the enemy if they attempted to use them as cover. The main purpose of the Lower Works was to 'give time, by an Alarm for the Garrison to get under Arms' and 'to throw Obstructions in the Way, in case of their Approach'. Most damning was his contention that 'I take no Notice of the advanced fleches or the Guns placed in them, as they were never intended as points of defense'.[5] Mercer thought, as did Marshal upon his arrival at Stony Point, that the Lower Work fleches and the deployment of artillery within them was a temporary measure intended to protect position while the Upper Works were completed, rather than permanent positions that required a full throated defense. Mercer also admits he never had a conversation with Lieutenant Colonel Johnson about the defenses in general and the intent of the Lower Works in particular. Nor did he have any discussions with the officer in charge of artillery concerning the role of the different artillery, specifically the use of the howitzer to protect the left flank.

The British were also aware that both the north and south Hudson River shorelines were rather shallow. Along the north shore at low tide the water was approximately 4 feet deep and somewhat shallower along the southern shore. Lieutenant Marshal believed despite the shallow water along the northern shore the rugged nature of the hillside between the Lower and Upper abatis would have made an attack through this area difficult. The posting of the naval vessels along both flanks reflected the continuing concern about the vulnerability of those approaches around the Lower Works. Despite the presence of the ships posted to protect both the north and south approaches there was some doubt about their overall effectiveness. The steepness of the hillside, coupled with limited ability to elevate its guns, would have significantly impacted the *Vulture's* ability to defend against an attack.

The southern shoreline, extending some distance out into Haverstraw Bay, provided an even more shallow depth at low tide, perhaps one foot, while at high tide it was estimated as waist deep. The bottom was described as a mix of sand and rocks, making walking over it less strenuous. Only the Lower Works abatis extended to the waterline in the area of the shallow shoreline. The shoreline fell away near the Upper Works abatis, restricting access from the river. An 8-inch mortar, which Robertson believed could strike targets anywhere along the southern hillside was placed behind the Upper Works abatis in a separate fleche. In addition an 18lb and 24lb gun were deployed within Upper Works parapet, although there was a difference of opinion between the British engineers as to whether these guns could even effectively protect the hillside to their front.

While there was some consideration given to the possibility of a night attack, the overall design of defenses appear to have assumed a daylight assault. Fire beacons were recommended by various engineers to be used to

---

5   Quoted in Loprieno, *Enterprise in Contemplation*, pp.247-248.

illuminate the vulnerable flanks. The artillery also had available fireballs, a shell made from a combination of gunpowder, sulphur, saltpeter, and pitch, which would ignite after being fired and provided temporary illumination. Neither option was employed during the American attack.

View from Stony Point south over Haverstraw Bay (Author's photo).

As midnight on 15 July approached, the British garrison at Stony Point found themselves defending a series of defensive fortifications too extensive to adequately man with the troops available. The abatis, which formed the main lines of resistance for both the Lower and Upper Works were, in places, thin and weakly secured. The abatis for the Lower Works could be flanked on both north and south by troops moving along the shoreline and the ships intended to defend against this movement had been withdrawn due to unfavorable winds. The artillery was without adequate ammunition and lacked a cohesive plan for how to react to a nighttime attack. The guns that defended the Upper Works were limited in their ability to provide complete coverage against the likely avenues of enemy approach and the defenses on the hilltop lacked all around fortifications, leaving them vulnerable to being outflanked. Overall the defenses were designed to respond to a daylight attack and very little consideration had been given to a night assault.

6

Anthony Wayne and the Creation of the Light Infantry Corps

At the time of the American Revolution, the major European military powers regularly created light infantry units intended to operate either as part of a parent unit or independently. These troops were organized and trained in a manner that allowed them greater flexibility to perform a range of functions that regular line units were not able to undertake, such as scouting and operating in looser formations. These looser formations often were used to engage formed enemy units in exchanges of musket fire. Because they operated in open order the light infantry were able to take advantage of cover provided by terrain or objects such as walls, while their targets stood in massed formation, usually in the open, providing convenient targets. The French and British all incorporated a company of light infantry as part of the organization of their regular regiments. These companies could be detached to operate independently or combined with similar companies from other regiments to create larger units. The German states organized *Jaeger* battalions, which normally operated separately from regular line regiments. Unlike their European counterparts the *Jaegers* were armed with rifles rather than the standard infantry muskets.

Each British regiment was composed of ten companies, including a company each of light infantry and grenadiers. The British considered these companies elite units and typically combined the light infantry and grenadier companies from different regiments into composite battalions. The light infantry formations were utilized in a variety of roles ranging from scouting and skirmishing to assault troops, depending on circumstances. British light infantry exhibited specific characteristics that contributed to their success. These included self-reliance, skill at adapting to their physical environment, and a high degree of adaptability and flexibility to respond to unexpected conditions.

Beginning with its creation in 1775 the Continental Army always had available a force of troops that functioned in many ways as did light infantry. Many of the American colonists who responded to the call to assemble an army in the aftermath of the battles around Boston in late 1775 were members of militias. The Colonial militia were organized in villages or counties and had rudimentary military training but were largely unfamiliar with traditional European formations and tactics. Another important source of militia came from pioneers living closer to the western and northern frontiers, which were largely mountainous and sparsely settled. These settlers were more likely to be familiar with hunting and most were armed with rifles, particularly the Pennsylvania rifle. The rifle was well suited to the preferred tactics of light infantry, operating in loose formations, while taking advantage of available cover. Although rifles had a longer range and were more accurate than muskets they took longer to load and lacked a bayonet, making these troops vulnerable to an enemy able to close with them quickly.

During 1775 and early 1776 the New England army gathering around Boston was composed of a polyglot of units from the surrounding states, organized in a variety of formations. It was not until 14 June 1776 that the Continental Congress passed legislation that attempted to standardize the organization. One of the acts taken by the Congress was to raise ten companies of riflemen, intended to act as light infantry for the larger army besieging Boston. Congress authorized each company to be made up of 80 men and directed that six companies be recruited from Pennsylvania, two each from Maryland and Virginia. The initial response from Pennsylvania was so great that two additional companies were authorized followed quickly by a third, resulting in a total of thirteen companies joining Washington's army outside Boston. Three rifle companies, including a Virginia company commanded by Colonel Daniel Morgan, were detached to accompany the forces assigned to Colonel Benedict Arnold to reinforce the Canadian invasion.

On 4 November 1776 Congress finalized the recommended organization of American infantry, mandating that each regiment should include eight companies, each totaling approximately 90 men. The Pennsylvania rifle companies, reorganized into a single regiment, were supplemented by the companies from Virginia and Maryland. Although Congress had stipulated an organizational structure for units in Continental service, individual states continued to modify as they saw fit. Virginia organized their regiment with ten companies and Colonel Daniel Morgan organized the 11th Virginia as a rifle regiment, incorporating companies from the original Virginia and Maryland rifle units. Morgan's 11th Virginia was the nucleus for the formation of a provisional rifle corps, assigned in June 1777 to serve as light infantry in the Northern Department. Morgan's troops were joined by a provisional light infantry battalion of 300 men in five companies commanded by Major Henry Dearborn. Dearborn's light infantry fought alongside Morgan's riflemen in the Saratoga campaign, both playing lead roles in the battles that led to the surrender of Burgoyne's army in October 1777.

On 28 August 1777, with Morgan's unit assigned to the Northern Department, Washington ordered the formation of a corps of light infantry, composed of a provisional company of 117 men drawn from each brigade. Two days later Washington assigned Brigadier General William Maxwell to command the corps and, writing to John Hancock, observed, 'sensible to the advantages of Light Troops, I have formed a Corps under the command of a

Brigadier, by drafting a Hundred from each Brigade, which is to be constantly near the Enemy and to give 'em every possible annoyance'.[1]

Since the structure of regular infantry regiments did not include a light infantry company, unlike their British counterparts, brigade and regimental officers were ordered to select men well suited to the role of light infantry for assignment. Reflecting this process the light infantry units were sometimes referred to as 'select men'.

In the aftermath of the 1777 campaign Washington requested advice from his senior generals on the organization of the army. Major General Nathaniel Greene outlined a proposed a major restructuring of the Continental Army and made specific reference to the establishment of formal light infantry companies, writing:

> Upon this establishment there will be twenty nine Commissioned Officers, forty eight non-commissioned, & five hundred and four rank and file. Each company will consist of fifty six privates—One Company should be a light Infantry Company, to act either with or without the regiment, as the nature of the service shall require. The light infantry to be always filled from the regiment, those serving in the light infantry companies upon good behaviour to be promoted to Serjeants, as vacancies happen in the Regiment. Experience has shewn us how necessary a good body of light infantry are. A good Corps of chosen troops, may by acting together give a favourable turn to an action that could not be obtained if they were dispersed among the regiments at large. In almost every action there is but a very small proportion of the Army that engages, the rest stand ready to support them, and the fate of the day commonly declares in favour of those who push their advantages in the first of the action, and by a judicious disposition secure what they have gained.[2]

Acting in part of Greene's recommendation, in January 1778 Washington proposed to modify the organization of infantry regiments and recommended the inclusion of a light infantry company as part of the regimental structure. Congress resolved in its new establishment of the army on 27 May 'That each batallion of infantry shall consist of nine companies, one of which shall be of light infantry; the light infantry to be kept complete by drafts from the batallion, and organized during the campaign into corps of light infantry'.[3]

The British evacuation of Philadelphia in June 1778 led Washington to order on 24 June that each brigade furnish an 'active spirited Officer and twenty-five of it's [sic] best marksmen'[4] The men were assigned to Colonel Morgan's 11th Virginia rifle regiment and tasked to harass the flanks of the retreating British columns. These marksmen were not necessarily part of the regimental light infantry companies since in an appendage to the General Orders Washington ordered the light infantry companies of the North Carolina brigade to join Morgan, superseding the directive for twenty five

---

1   Washington Hancock, 30 August 1777, *Founders Online,* National Archives.
2   Greene to Washington January 1778, *Founders Online,* National Archives.
3   Quoted in Worthington Chauncey Ford et al. (eds.) *Journals of the Continental Congress, 1774-1789* (Washington, D.C.: Washington Printing Office, 1904-37), Vol.11, pp.538-39.
4   General Orders, 22 June 1778, *Founders Online,* National Archives.

men On the same date Washington formally organized the remaining light infantry companies into a corps, totaling approximately 1,500 men, under the command of Brigadier General Charles Scott on 24 June. Lieutenant Colonel Henry Dearborn wrote that 'a detachment of 1500 Pick'd men was taken to Day from the army to be Commanded by Brigadier Genrl. Scott who are to act as Light Infantry'.[5] Washington ordered Scott to 'fall in with the enemy's left flank and rear, and give them all the annoyance in your power'.[6]

In the confusion that characterized the Battle of Monmouth, 28 June 1778, Scott's light infantry corps was in the vanguard of the American advance but during the subsequent withdrawal was utilized like a regular infantry formations. Scott's force did not particularly distinguish itself during the battle and in the aftermath of the action Washington may have concluded that the ad hoc nature of the light infantry formations was to blame. Thrown together to form temporary units with men and officers unfamiliar to one another and with no prior experience training together it was difficult to expect the light infantry to perform as an elite unit. Private Joseph Plumb Martin, a member of the 1778 light infantry, recounted, 'the duties of the Light Infantry is the hardest, while in the field, of any troops in the army, if there is any *hardest* about it. During the time the army keeps the field they are always on the lines near the enemy, and consequently always on alert, constantly on watch'.[7]

Brigadier General Scott was again tapped to lead the light infantry corps on 8 August when Washington ordered the creation of the formation 'for the Safety and Ease of the Army and to be in greater to attack or repel the enemy'.[8] In his order Washington implied that this action was temporary in nature, pending a more complete implementation of the Congressional resolution of 27 May, which made specific reference to the creation of a light infantry corps. Scott continued to command the light corps until November 1778 when he retired from the army due to reasons of ill health. Washington appointed Colonel David Henley to command the corps until the end of the month, at which time the army was assigned to enter winter cantonments and the light infantry companies were ordered to return to their parent units.

As Washington responded to a possible British advance up the Hudson Valley towards West Point in early 1779 he had already begun to consider reassembling the corps of light infantry. Brigadier General Anthony Wayne, who had taken a leave of absence from the army at the conclusion of the 1778 campaign, wrote to Washington on 10 February 1779 offering his services for the upcoming campaign season. Rather than requesting reappointment to his previous command Wayne asked to be considered to lead the light corps. Wayne's interest in command of the light infantry was not new to Washington. On 30 May 1778, as Washington anticipated the British evacuation of Philadelphia, Wayne wrote to Washington and asked his consideration for command of the light corps. Rather than grant Wayne's request Washington

---

5   Lloyd A. Brown and Howard H. Peckham (eds.), *Revolutionary War Journals of Henry Dearborn, 1775–1783*. (Chicago: Canton Club, 1939) p.124.

6   Washington to Scott, 24 June 1778, *Founders Online*, National Archives.

7   James Kirby Martin, *Ordinary Courage, The Revolutionary War Adventures of Joseph Plumb Martin* (New York: St James, 1993), p.82.

8   General Orders, 8 August 1778, *Founders Online,* National Archives.

appointed to Wayne to a divisional command, where he played a significant role in the battle of Monmouth.

Considering Wayne's recent request to lead the light infantry Washington responded quickly on 17 February, 'cheerfully' accepting his offer once circumstances allowed for the creation of the light corps. With his appointment Washington elevated an aggressive commander, who had proven his resolve and valor, into a position that would play a critical role in the coming campaign, allowing Wayne to expiate any lingering doubts about his competence. Washington also recognized in Wayne a leader who shared his desire to strike at the enemy and who was willing to take risks.

Anthony Wayne was born on New Year's Day, 1745 in Easttown, in Chester County, Pennsylvania. Wayne's grandfather, also named Anthony, had served in the British Army and fought at the Battle of the Boyne in 1690. The senior Wayne immigrated to Pennsylvania in 1722 and settled in Chester County. His youngest son, Isaac, accumulated large land holdings and success as a farmer. After several years of education under the guidance of his uncle Gilbert, Anthony was enrolled in the Philadelphia Academy. By age 18 Wayne was a trained surveyor working in the Pennsylvania frontier and in Nova Scotia. In 1766 he married and by 1774 had established a large farm and tannery in Wayneboro in Chester County. As Britain and her American Colonies lurched towards an open break, Wayne was active as a member of the Pennsylvania Provincial Convention and, in 1775, served on the County Committees of Safety and Correspondence.

At the same time Wayne, who had a lifelong interest in military science, began actively recruiting the Fourth Pennsylvania Battalion and was subsequently elected its colonel. Wayne and the Fourth Pennsylvania Battalion were assigned to serve in the Northern Army under General John Sullivan. On 8 June 1776 the Americans were routed by British forces and in the confused retreat Wayne, although slightly wounded, commanded the American rearguard. When the American Army began to retreat from Canada Wayne assumed command of the Pennsylvania brigade in place of senior officers that had been captured or wounded. Wayne spent the remainder of 1776 stationed at Fort Ticonderoga and given command of the Fort on 18 November. As fort commander Wayne addressed a wide range of issues, including lack of supplies, rampant disease and widespread desertions. Promoted to brigadier general on 21 February, 1777 Wayne was ordered to join the American Army at Morristown, New Jersey on 12 April. Wayne was given command of a division composed of eight regiments, 1,700 men, of the newly formed Pennsylvania Line.

Wayne and his division fought at Brandywine, 11 September 1777 part of the Continental Army defending Chad's Ford against British and Hessian troops. In the aftermath of the Battle of Brandywine Washington ordered the Continental Army to retire across the Schuylkill River, through Philadelphia, and occupy a position that allowed him to protect both Philadelphia and his supply base at Reading, Pennsylvania. Due to shortages of wagons for transport of his wounded and supplies, Howe's British Army remained deployed near the Brandywine battlefield. Washington re-crossed the Schuylkill hoping to challenge Howe, who responded in kind by advancing to engage the Americans. On 16 September a confused action took place near White Horse Tavern, with Washington assigning Wayne to lead the advance guard and ordering him to slow the British advance while he deployed the Continental Army for battle. Wayne commanded the 1st and 2nd Pennsylvania Brigades, composed of Continental regulars, and several Pennsylvania militia regiments. Wayne's forces engaged the advancing British and Hessians and skirmished throughout the early afternoon while Washington struggled to get the main American Army in place. Realizing his forces would be unable to deploy in time Washington ordered a retreat just as a terrific rainstorm unleased itself over the battlefield. The torrential rain ruined the powder and rendered muskets unusable, forcing Howe and Washington to break off the engagement.

Washington quickly retired across the Schuylkill River but left Wayne and his Pennsylvania Division near Howe's troops, ordering him to harass the British baggage train as the main army advanced towards Philadelphia. At the same time Washington ordered the select men from each brigade to reform the light corps under Brigadier General Maxwell and suggested to Wayne that he cooperate if possible with the light corps. Washington closed his letter to Wayne requesting information on his movements and included an all too prophetic note, cautioning Wayne to 'take care of Ambuscades'.[9]

Anthony Wayne, by Alonzo Chappel, 1857 (Library of Congress).

On 19 September Wayne established his camp near the Paoli Tavern. His force consisted of eight Pennsylvania Regiments, Hartley's Regiment, four cannon, and a number of Continental Dragoons, totaling approximately 1,500 men. Brigadier General William Smallwood, with 2,000 Maryland militia and several cannon, was marching to join Wayne and was expected to arrive sometime on 20 September. Although Paoli Tavern was only four miles from the British camp at Tredyffrin, Wayne believed the British were unaware of his location. For his part Howe was well aware of Wayne's location, his mission, and the composition of his force. With this information Howe recognized an opportunity to strike at Wayne and ordered Major General Charles Grey to undertake the attack.

Early on 19 September Wayne updated Washington, noting that he had marched to within one half mile of the British camp but found Howe had not stirred and there was no opportunity for his men to strike the British. On 20 September, while waiting for Smallwood to arrive, Wayne and his staff continued to probe the British camp and collect intelligence. By the evening of 20 September Wayne and his senior officers were aware that the British were planning on attacking their forces, probably during the coming night. Further information about a probable British attack was provided around 8:00 pm by a local resident. This latest information confirmed earlier intelligence

9   Washington to Wayne, 18 September 1777, *Founders Online,* National Archives.

and Wayne was faced with a difficult decision. Prudence suggested he move his camp, but he was still expecting Smallwood's militia force. Inexplicably, rather than focus on the anticipated British attack, Wayne later explained his decision to stay, in part, was based on an belief that Howe was planning to march the next day. Wayne appears to have made plans intended to respond to Howe's march and fulfill Washington's order to harass the British baggage train rather than address the more immediate possibility of an attack on his camp:

> I had the fullest and Clearest Advice that the Enemy would March that Morning at 2 OClock for the River Schuylkill. In Consequence of that Advice I had Reconnoitered a Road leading Immediately along the Right flank of the Enemy and that in Company with Coll. Humpton and Hartley and had the men laying on their arms to Move as soon as Gen. Smallwood should arrive.[10]

On 20 September Wayne had established four picket posts at select locations leading to their camp. With the most recent information of a British attack, two additional pickets were established. Sometime before midnight Wayne ordered twelve mounted dragoons to reinforce the pickets. These mounted pickets, referred to as videttes, were distributed among the already established locations.

Marching from the British camp at 10.00 pm, Grey's force included the 2nd Light Infantry Battalion, composed of the light companies of 13 regiments, the 42nd Highlanders and 44th Foot, totaling 1,200 men. Also included in Grey's force were 12 cavalry from the 16th Light Dragoons. Another British force, commanded by Colonel Thomas Musgrave, composed of the 40th and 55th Foot left the British camp at 11:00 pm and deployed on the Lancaster Road to block the possible retreat of Wayne's men to the east.

Grey wished to ensure the Americans were not warned of their approach by an accidental discharge of a musket. He ordered all flints removed from the British muskets, which would eliminate any possible accidental discharge and require his men to use only their bayonets to fight the Americans. The commander of the 2nd Light Infantry, Major Maitland, argued his highly disciplined light infantry could be relied upon to obey orders not to fire and so were allowed to carry loaded muskets.

Despite the precautions against alerting Wayne's forces the British soon encountered a series of American cavalry videttes, which fired at the intruders and retreated to inform Wayne of the enemy advance. Wayne was alert to the British threat soon after the first contact was reported and issued orders for his men to form. At this point Wayne only knew that his videttes had tangled with British cavalry but suspected a larger force was in the vicinity.

Despite having several local guides directing them as the British column reached the Warren Tavern they found themselves uncertain of the route to Wayne's camp. A local blacksmith, pressed into service, led the British along the Lancaster Road rather than the Sugartown Road. Although both routes brought them into contact with the American camp a British attack from the Sugartown Road would have driven Wayne's men into towards Musgrave's

---

10 Thomas J. McGuire, *Battle of Paoli* (Mechanicsburg: Stackpole Books, 2000), p.86.

blocking force and might have resulted in the complete destruction of Wayne's Division. As they advanced along the Lancaster Road the British overran a vidette from the 4th Pennsylvania, which fired a ineffective volley before being overwhelmed.

By this time the American camp was alive to the danger. Major Francis Mentges of the 11th Pennsylvania Regiment later testified that 'At about 12 o'clock Genl. Wayne came Riding along in the Rear of the 2d Brigade Calling out "Turn out my Boys, the Lads are Comeing, we gave them a push with the Bayonet through the Smoak". The Troops turned out as quick as Could be Expected and Formed by Platoons, in less than five Minutes'.[11]

Wayne's two brigades formed, Colonel Richard Humpton's 2nd Brigade on the left and Colonel Thomas Hartley's 1st Brigade on the right, both brigades facing the Lancaster Road. On the far right of the American line four cannon were deployed. As a light rain began to fall Wayne ordered his men to begin to withdraw to the left, away from the increasing musket fire erupting on the right. The American artillery limbered and followed by a number of supply wagons quickly moved towards the Sugartown Road. To protect his withdrawal Wayne ordered the 1st Pennsylvania to advance and deploy in a wooded area on the right.

The British continued their relentless advance in silence, without returning the fire from the pickets they encountered. The 2nd Light Infantry quickly overran several of the pickets. In the ensuing confusion Wayne noticed that for unknown reasons the withdrawal had ground to a halt. Wayne sent repeated orders to resume the withdrawal without success. Finally Wayne rode forward to find the cause of the delay. While Wayne was trying to untangle his columns the British light infantry broke through the unsteady 1st Pennsylvania, driving them out of the woods and back in to the camp. The disordered retreat of the 1st Pennsylvania brought them and the pursuing 2nd Light Infantry towards the rear of the 2nd Brigade column. As the 2nd Light Infantry surged forward they overlapped the narrow frontage of the rear of the American column. The light from the burning camp fires, made hazy by the smoke from the discharge of muskets, coupled with the shouts of the attacking British created panic and confusion among the Americans.

As the 2nd Light Infantry surrounded the rear of the American column, the cavalry of the 16th Light Dragoons and infantry from the 44th Foot joined the melee. This force moved up along the American column, through the abandoned campsite, pausing to strike at the Continentals milling in confusion.

As the battle continued Wayne organized several rearguards to slow the British advance and protect those men still in danger. For a large portion of his division organized resistance was futile and men escaped individually and in small groups as best they could. The darkness of night, which initially gave an advantage to the British attackers now gave protection to the defenders.

At about midnight, and a mile west of the American camp, Smallwood's force of Maryland militia was marching to join Wayne. Smallwood halted his column as the sounds of battle at Wayne's camp echoed in the night air. Smallwood immediately retreated to the west and deployed on higher

---

11   Quoted in McGuire, *Paoli*, p.101.

ground. Soon after posting his men groups of American stragglers followed by the lead elements of the British 2nd Light Infantry began to appear along their front. Emboldened by their success in routing Wayne's men the British light infantry began to fire at the militia line. At the approach of the British infantry the militia, largely untrained and always uncomfortable at the sudden appearance of the enemy at night, fled in panic. Smallwood's men tumbled back west to White Horse Tavern which Wayne had designated as the rallying point for his men and Smallwood's command.

The British victory was complete. At the cost of four dead and seven wounded they had scattered Wayne's two brigades and shattered the Maryland militia. American casualties were at least 53 dead, 72 taken prisoner, and numerous wounded, totaling a loss of 272 men. In addition the British captured several wagons loaded with supplies and ammunition. The Maryland militia, while suffering less than 10 killed, suffered the additional loss of over 1,000 men who deserted the colors and returned to their homes. Physically Wayne's men had been severely mauled and his command disordered, requiring time to rest and regroup. Psychologically the terror of the British assault and impact of the death and wounding of men by bayonet exceeded the physical losses. Although Wayne maintained his command had not been surprised and totally unprepared to defend their position he recognized how difficult it was for troops to respond in the confusion and panic in the midst of a night attack. Control was severely limited in the darkness, troops disoriented, unable to hear or respond to simple commands and all semblance of organization lost. The attacker had the initiative and could easily outmaneuver their opponents. When coupled with the exclusive use of bayonets, the tactic could be devastating.

On 22 September Wayne marched his decimated command northwest to the Jones Tavern, near Reading, Pennsylvania. One that day Wayne wrote to Washington to describe the events at Paoli. Wayne's description was at times extraordinarily understated, suggesting 'Part of the Division were a little scattered but are collecting fast' while in others wholly inaccurate, claiming 'We have saved all our Artillery, Ammunition and Stores'. Wayne mentioned the appearance of Smallwood's command but included no information about the collapse of the militia. He closed the note promising that 'As soon as we have refreshed our Troops for an Hour to Two, we shall follow the Enemy'.[12] Whether Wayne truly believed his division was capable of further action his statement belied the true nature of the state of his command.

Although Wayne sought to minimize the impact of his defeat at Paoli, members of his senior command were less sanguine. While Wayne marched his men on 24 September to re-join the main army Colonel Thomas Hartley, commander of the 2nd Brigade, accompanied the wounded to a hospital at Reading, Pennsylvania. At Reading Hartley had breakfast with John Adams and other members of Congress and was evidently critical of Wayne's leadership and decisions on the night of the attack. Writing sometime later Congressman Henry Laurens of South Carolina noted 'At Reading I

---

12   Wayne to Washington, 21 September 1777, *Founders Online,* National Archives.

learned of General Wayne's false step' and later referred to 'the unpardonable negligence of General Wayne'.[13]

Hartley was hardly alone in his criticism of Wayne. Over the next several days Wayne had confrontations with several officers including Colonel Richard Humpton, commander of the 1st Brigade. With both brigade commanders and several regimental commanders challenging his fitness Wayne demanded an inquiry into the events of that evening. Washington immediately granted Wayne's request, which seemed to have gratified Wayne's critics. Major Samuel Hay, whose 7th Pennsylvania had tried in vain to stem the tide of the British advance, wrote on 29 September, 'The officers of the division have protested against Gen Wayne's conduct, and lodged a complaint and requested a court martial, which his Excellency has promised they shall have'.[14]

The inquiry into Wayne's conduct at Paoli was convened on 13 October and focused on whether Wayne had acted in a timely manner to respond to the information he was provided of the imminent British attack. The tribunal, composed of senior officers, heard testimony from Wayne's subordinate officers and after two days of testimony rendered an opinion. The exact details of the tribunals findings have been lost but their conclusion must have suggested Wayne was culpable to some degree for the disaster, which did not satisfy Wayne's sense of honor. On 22 October he wrote Washington a long response, bitterly attacking the conduct of the inquiry and requesting a full court-martial to exonerate his behavior. During the formal court-martial, held on 25 October, Wayne provided a spirited defense of his conduct. On 1 November the panel issued an opinion fully vindicating Wayne's conduct. Soon afterwards a frustrated Colonel Daniel Broadhead, commander of the 8th Pennsylvania, complained to Major General Benjamin Lincoln that the 'Division has suffered greatly and that chiefly by the Conduct of Gl-W. Most of the officers are unhappy under his Command and as to my own part I have had very little satisfaction'.[15]

Testimony from various officers at both hearings attested to the confusion sown by the British attack. Lieutenant Colonel Adam Hubley, 10th Pennsylvania, recounted ' … before we could advance, any distance, the Enemy were upon us, in our rear, and with their charg'd Bayonets, we push'd forward and got into a field adjoining the One in which we were Attackted, [.] we endeavored to form Our Men, but found it impracticable, the Enemy being then, almost mix'd with us, at the same time calling out, No quarters &c'.[16]

With the British in possession of Philadelphia the focus on operations turned to the defense of the forts Mercer and Mifflin located along the Delaware River. Mifflin, located on Mud Island in the middle of the river and Mercer, at Red Bank on the New Jersey shore prevented British shipping from gaining access to Philadelphia, restricting Howe's ability to adequately supply his troops. Through the remainder of 1777 and into early 1778 Wayne

---

13 Quoted in McGuire, *Paoli*, p.165.
14 Quoted in McGuire, *Paoli*, p.167.
15 Quoted in McGuire, *Paoli*, p.183.
16 Quoted in McGuire, *Paoli*, p.210.

and his division operated as part of Washington's main Continental Army. On 22 October a strong force of Hessians was repulsed with heavy casualties in a failed assault on Fort Mercer. The Hessian commander Colonel Karl Von Donop was mortally wounded in the attack. A simultaneous attack on Fort Mifflin by British naval vessels was likewise turned back. In response these reverses Howe began to construct redoubts and artillery batteries on Carpenter Island, directly across a 500 yard channel from Fort Mifflin.

As was his practice during this period, Washington held a series of Councils of War with his senior generals to solicit their advice on a range of topic but focused primarily on possible strategies to respond to the British occupation of Philadelphia. On 26 October Washington issued a set of eight questions for response at a Council. The first question asked simply if it would be prudent to attempt to attack the enemy.

Wayne responded to Washington the next day, making an impassioned case for an immediate attack on the British. Wayne contended that 'if the Enemy are not Immediately Dislodged-all our Defenses and Shipping on the River will Inevitably fall into their hands'.[17] At the Council held on 29 October, consensus among the officers present was not to support a general action against the British. As part of their discussion the Council did agree that the forts should be reinforced.

As the British began construction of the battery on Carpenter Island another Council was held on 8 November. Washington told the group he anticipated an imminent attack on the forts and asked again whether, in that event, the army should attack the British lines around Philadelphia. The Council, including Wayne, voted unanimously against the army being deployed in support of the forts.

With the completion of their position on Carpenter Island the British began a bombardment of Fort Mifflin on 10 November. Brigadier General Richard Varnum, in overall command of both forts, wrote Washington in desperation on 11 November describing the destruction wrought by the British artillery and suggested the garrison be reduced. Washington replied the next day, recommending Varnum leave a small force defend the Fort as long as possible but that the remaining works be blown up or burned and the bulk of the garrison withdrawn. On 13 November Washington returned to the possibility of a raid suggesting to Varnum 'I think an Enterprise of a more active nature might be carried into execution in concert with a detachment from the Fleet, I mean a descent upon Province [Carpenter} Island for the purpose of spiking the Enemy's Cannon and levelling their batteries'.[18] Washington left the final decision to Varnum, who replied on 14 November rejecting the proposed action, 'An Attempt upon Province [Carpenter] Island is desirable, but impossible for us, who have no Troops, but fatigued ones, & those in less Force than the Enemy's upon that Place'.[19]

Recognizing Varnum's reservations about a possible a sortie against Carpenter Island Washington proposed a slightly scaled back effort on 15

---

17 Quoted in Charles J. Stille, *Major General Anthony Wayne and the Pennsylvania Line in the Continental Army* (Philadelphia: Lippincot Company, 1893), p.109.
18 Washington to Varnum, 13 November 1777, *Founders Online,* National Archives.
19 Varnum to Washington, 14 November 1777, *Founders Online,* National Archives.

November, noting 'that I proposed the ruin of the Enemys works as part of the end in view – yet I should be content if nothing more could be effected – to have only the Cannon of their Batteries or any part of them spiked up – a resolute body of Volunteers and picked men I still think might be employed with Success in this Undertaking – and tho the time gained by us and the Embarrassment occasioned the Enemy would not be so considerable as in the other case – yet it appears to me to be an attempt worth making – especially as by the means of Surprise, the Service might be done, before the Party could be opposed in force'.[20]

By the time Varnum received Washington's revised proposal the British were on the move and Varnum reported that he was going to evacuate the fort on the night of 15 November Fort Mercer was subsequently abandoned on 20 November.

It is unclear how much Wayne influenced Washington's continued interest in attacking the British works on Carpenter Island, but his frustration with the lack of aggressive action by the Continental Army is evident in a letter sent on 18 November to Richard Peters, Secretary to the Board of War. In it Wayne notes that Fort Mifflin had fallen and points out 'six weeks Investiture and no Attempt to raise the siege of that fort will scarcely be Credited at an Other day you'l ask what was the cause of this Supineness an over stretched caution, which is oftentimes attended with as fatal Consequences as too much rashness, the present, as well as some past events, full evinces the truth of this position'.[21]

In the letter Wayne claimed that Washington ordered him to collect information on the British positions on Carpenter Island and proposed to the Council of War an immediate attack to raise the siege of Fort Mifflin but his proposal was rejected by the Council. Rather than accept their judgement, Wayne contended that Washington made plans to move the main Continental Army to support an attack on Carpenter Island by Wayne's Division and Colonel Daniel Morgan's corps of riflemen. According to Wayne, the attack, intended to destroy the British works and disable their cannon, was scheduled for 16 November but the evacuation of the fort on the night of 15 November resulted in the attack being canceled. In a foreshadowing of the attack on Stony Point Wayne wrote, 'there was some Difficulty, as well as Danger in the Attempt-but the success depended more on the fortitude of the Troops, as the Vigor with which the Attack was made-than upon numbers'.[22]

Despite Wayne's obvious disappointment over the loss of the Delaware River forts he continued to encourage Washington to consider an offensive against the British. At a Council of War on 24 November Brigadier General John Cadwalader presented Washington and his senior generals with a detailed proposal for attacking Philadelphia within the week. The responses sent to Washington varied between outright rejection and conditional support. Although Cadwalader's timetable was much too aggressive, Washington encouraged his subordinates to consider Cadwalader's plan or other options for engaging the British. On 3 December Washington reminded the generals

---

20 Washington to Varnum, 15 November 1777, *Founders Online,* National Archives.
21 Quoted in Stille, *Anthony Wayne*, p.105.
22 Quoted in Stille, *Anthony Wayne*, p.105.

he had requested their opinions about both a winter campaign and an attack on Philadelphia. At the same time as he was assessing the feasibility of attacking the British, Washington asked the generals for their thoughts about where to go into winter quarters. On 30 November Washington ask for their recommendation on three possible locations. The first option proposed establishing camps west of Philadelphia, along a line between Lancaster and Reading, Pennsylvania. The second option was to winter around Wilmington, Delaware, east of Philadelphia. The final option was to make camp at Valley Forge.

The opinions of the generals on winter quarters were more divided than their response to the suggested attack on Philadelphia. The majority supported the Lancaster to Reading proposal, while almost as many, including Wayne, voted for Wilmington. Wayne argued against the Lancaster option, suggesting the location was too far, 60 miles, from the enemy's base at Philadelphia. In this position Washington would be unable to counter British movements in New Jersey and along the Eastern Shore. Wayne supported Wilmington, claiming 'the position is such as to give the Enemy the Greatest Annoyance – with the least fatigue to your own troops'.[23]

Hoping for as clear a consensus as they had given him on the prospect of attacking Philadelphia Washington wrote in frustration to Joseph Reed on 2 December, asking to meet with him and complaining 'I am abt fixing the Winter cantonments of this army and find so many and such capitol objections to each mode proposed, that I am exceedingly embarrassed, not only by the advice given to me, but in my own judgement'.[24]

With regard to the idea of a winter campaign Wayne appeared to agree with the majority of his fellow officers that the Continental Army was not prepared for such an undertaking, although, as usual Wayne added a caveat. If wintering at Wilmington or within 20 miles west of Philadelphia could be considered a winter campaign he would support the proposal.

As if Washington did not have his hands already full, a Congressional committee arrived at the Whitemarsh camp on 28 November, to discuss Cadwalader's proposal to attack Philadelphia. Washington passed along the negative responses of the generals to both the proposal to attack Philadelphia and engage in a winter campaign. These discussions were interrupted on 4 December as the British Army stirred from Philadelphia, advancing towards Washington at Whitemarsh. On 7 December Colonel Morgan's Rifle Corps, supported by a large force of militia, fought an inconclusive action against British light infantry at Edge Hill. Washington fully expected a general engagement the next day but inexplicably Howe ordered the British Army to return to Philadelphia. Returning to their deliberations the Congressional committee prepared a report on 10 December which concluded any an attack on Philadelphia 'under the current circumstances of the Army, attended with such a variety of difficulties as to render it ineligible'.[25] With the question of further offensive actions resolved Washington directed the Army into winter

---

23 Wayne to Washington, 1 December 1777, *Founders Online,* National Archives.
24 Washington to Reed, 2 December 1777, *Founders Online,* National Archives.
25 Continental Congress Camp Committee to Washington, 10 December 1777, *Founders Online,* National Archives.

quarters. Despite gaining the support of only Major General Lord Sterling Washington opted to establish his winter quarters in the 'Great Valley' near a burnt out iron works, Valley Forge.

Wayne spent the first half of 1778, looking after the welfare of his men, doing battle with officials in various commissary departments, trying to procure clothes, shoes and weapons. When not engaged in struggles over supplies with the Quartermaster General Wayne and his men were dispatched into New Jersey in search of cattle. With June came the British withdrawal from Philadelphia and Washington, anxious to regain the strategic initiative, prepared to engage the British as they moved towards New York. Towards that end Washington convened a Council on War on 24 June, 1778 and to his consternation the majority of his senior officers advised against bringing on a general action with Clinton, who had replaced Howe as the overall British commander. Wayne once again found himself in a distinct minority, advocating for an immediate attack on the British, while the other officers either recommended restraint or cautious half measures. In this case he was joined by Greene and Lafayette in suggesting an aggressive attack on Clinton's baggage train. On 28 June Washington engaged Clinton at Monmouth, New Jersey. In a day of confused fighting under intense heat Wayne's Pennsylvania Division fought throughout the day. Wayne's men engaged the British as part of the initial American attack, acted as a rearguard during the precipitous retreat, and were the last units to engage the British at the end of the day as Clinton retreated from the field.

Wayne spent the remainder of 1778 with his men at the Middlebrook encampment, struggling to replace losses through recruitment, secure replacement clothing and shoes for his men, and keep them fed. Wayne applied for and was given a leave of absence in February, 1779, handing over command of the Pennsylvania Division to Major General Arthur St. Clair. During this leave Wayne turned his attention to command of the light corps and applied again to Washington to command the light corps.

With Washington's reply of 12 February 1779 promising him command of the light corps Wayne remained on leave telling Washington he needed to address long overdue private matters but offered to rejoin the army if needed to assist in the formation of the light corps. Washington responded in early March that he would recall Wayne at some point in the future. Several months later on 18 May, after hearing nothing from Washington, Wayne let Washington know he had put his personal affairs in order and again offered to rejoin the army to assist in organizing the light corps. That Wayne was not directly involved in the creation of the light corps may have resulted from his own recommendation. With the news that Wayne would command the light corps several officers from his from his former command, the Pennsylvania line, requested transfer and appointment. In response Wayne wrote Washington 10 May, 'I had better be absent while the corps is being organized, lest it be supposed, however erroneously, that partiality of mine for certain officers had tended to bring them into the corps'.[26]

---

26   Quoted in James Barnes, *The Hero of Stony Point, Anthony Wayne* (New York: D. Appleton, 1916), p.34.

Recognizing that the Continental Army would be required to respond soon to British movements Wayne wrote Washington again on 30 May, expressing some frustration that he had 'not heard whether the Arrangement has yet taken place by which a light Corps was to be formed … the is now arrived when that Corps will be wanted to act in the field – all I wish is to be made one of the number'.[27]

Some time in early June, as he issued orders for the army to march from Middlebrook into Smith's Clove, Washington sent a message to Wayne in Philadelphia to rejoin the army to take command of the light corps but that note was somehow lost and Wayne did not hear from Washington again until 21 June. Washington's note was short and direct, 'I request that you join the Army as soon as you can'. Wayne set out at once for Washington's headquarters in Smith's Clove.

On 12 June Washington issued a general order establishing the light infantry corps, composed of three divisions of troops from Virginia, Maryland, and Pennsylvania regiments. Washington cautioned the regimental officers selecting the men to 'be particularly careful in the choice of men, which is a duty, the good of the service, and the credit of their credit of their respective regiments'.[28] The 13 Virginia regiments were ordered to provide 247 men, Maryland's seven regiments to contribute 164, and the eight Pennsylvania regiments, along with a Delaware regiment, 246 men, for a total of 657. The troops were organized into 16 companies, and each regiment was also responsible for nomination of one captain, a lieutenant, and three sergeants for each company. With the addition of the company officers the light infantry corps totaled 737.

The organization of the corps was further refined on 15 June when they were organized into four battalions, each composed of four companies. The battalions were then paired to form two regiments.

One regiment was commanded by Colonel Richard Butler. Butler, 36, was born in Ireland but moved to Pennsylvania with his family at age five. His father was a gunsmith and quickly learned to produce the Pennsylvania long rifle. The family moved from Lancaster to the western frontier at Carlisle, Pennsylvania where Butler became an acquaintance of Daniel Morgan. Butler was commissioned a major in 1776 and joined Morgan's rifle corps for the Saratoga campaign. Made a lieutenant colonel in 1777 Butler was given temporary command of the light infantry corps in Wayne's absence. Butler had commanded light infantry in the previous campaigns, Private Joseph Plumb Martin, serving in the 1778 corps of light infantry noted:

> [O]ur regiment was commanded by a Colonel Butler, a Pennsylvanian … he was a brave officer, but a fiery austere hothead. Whenever he had a dispute with a brother officer, and that was pretty often, he would never resort to pistols or swords, but always to his fists. I have more than once or twice seen him with a 'black eye' and have seen other officers that he had honored with the same badge.[29]

---

27 Wayne to Washington, 30 May 1778, *Founders Online*, National Archives.
28 General Orders, 12 June 1779, *Founders Online,* National Archives.
29 Martin, *Ordinary Courage*, p.82.

Major John Steward, 23, commanded four companies of Maryland light infantry which composed one of the two battalions of Butler's regiment. Stewart, born into a Quaker family in Calvert County, Maryland joined Washington's army in1776 as a member of Maryland's Fifth Independent Company. Steward was a veteran of the major battles of 1776, and fought as part of the rearguard that protected the Continental Army's withdrawal from Long Island. In April, 1777 Stewart was promoted to major in the 2nd Maryland Regiment. Steward was captured in August, 1777 during an abortive raid against the British on Staten Island, but escaped a month later and rejoined his regiment.

The second battalion of Butler's regiment was composed of four Pennsylvania companies and commanded by Lieutenant Colonel Samuel Hay. Hay, 39, had served with the Continental Army since January, 1776, assigned to several different Pennsylvania regiments. In the course of his service with the Pennsylvania line he had served extensively under Wayne.

The second regiment of light infantry was assigned to Colonel Christian Febiger, 34. Febiger was born in Denmark in 1746, educated at a military school in Copenhagen, and served in the Danish Army in the West Indies. After an extended visit to the American Colonies Febiger immigrated to Boston in 1772, married, and became a successful merchant. He joined a Massachusetts militia regiment after the outbreak of hostilities in 1775, fought at Bunker Hill, and was a member of Colonel Benedict Arnold's Quebec expedition. He was captured during the assault on Quebec and subsequently paroled. He was appointed lieutenant colonel in November 1776 and assigned to Colonel Morgan's 11th Virginia. Febiger fought at Brandywine and was made colonel of the 2nd Virginia on 26 September, 1777. After fighting at Germantown and enduring the winter at Valley Forge Febiger led his regiment at Monmouth.

Serving under Febiger and commanding a battalion of four companies from Virginia, Major Thomas Posey, 29, was a veteran of the Saratoga campaign, serving in a company of Virginia riflemen with Colonel Morgan's Rifle Corps. Born in 1750 in Virginia, Posey served in Lord Dunmore's army and fought at the Battle of Point Pleasant in 1774. Joining the 7th Virginia as a captain in 1775 Posey was promoted to major in 1778 Posey led the Rifle Corps in the expedition against Indians in Wyoming Valley, New York before being assigned to command of the 11th Virginia.

Febiger's second battalion was commanded by Lieutenant Colonel Francois-Louis Tesseidre, Marquis de Fleury. Fleury's battalion was composed of two companies of Virginia and two companies of Pennsylvania troops. Born in France in 1749, Fleury joined the French Army in 1768 and volunteered for service in America. Fleury fought at Brandywine and was wounded at Germantown before playing a key role in the defense of Fort Mifflin in November, 1777, where he was wounded. In 1778 Fleury fought at both Monmouth and Rhode Island as an aide to Major General von Steuben.

As a group, Wayne's senior officers were seasoned and battle tested. In one capacity or another they had all displayed bravery and initiative under fire. All but Fleury had served in a light infantry or rifle unit and were familiar with the unique demands expected of their men. Fleury brought his own unique skills as a trained engineer, and experience in assaults on fortified places. Most of them had served together in the Saratoga campaign or as members of the Pennsylvania line. As Wayne had expected, the most experienced veterans from the Pennsylvania regiments had volunteered for a place in the light infantry. The same was true of the men from Maryland and Virginia.

Adjutant General Alexander Scammell, a former commander of a New Hampshire regiment and veteran of the Saratoga campaign was given responsibility by Washington to administer the formation and organization of the Corps. After a 15 June inspection Scammell reported to Washington as follows:

> The above companies almost to a man are composed of proper sized well built men from five seven to five feet nine inches high, who have been in Actual Service two, three and Some almost four years, a very few excepted, who are natives. Four only out of the sixteen companies were ordered to be exchanged for better men. The arms and accoutrements (except in the 8th Va. Regiment) are in good order and complete. A few of the Men are in want of shoes who were absent at the last draught. The Baron Steuben is concerting measures with the officers of the Virginia and Pennsylvania Lines to have their three incomplete companies filled up immediately.[30]

On 21 June Washington ordered that six drumers and fifers each from the Virginia and Pennsylvania regiments and four from the Maryland regiments be assigned immediately to the light infantry corps. On that day he also ordered Colonel Richard Butler, in temporary command of the corps in Wayne's absence, to move the corps to a location near Fort Montgomery. The orders included a map of the area and specific instructions of where Butler was to place his pickets to warn of a British attack. Washington wrote Butler again on 24 June, cautioning him to be vigilant with regard to preventing desertion. Washington's concern about a possible British attack against the West Point forts was heightened with news from Butler that his men had observed an enemy force, estimated at 400 in strength, across the Hudson. From the detail Washington included in his orders it appears he was taking a very keen interest in the Light Corps.

Despite his best efforts not everyone was happy with Washington's selection of Wayne to lead the Light Corps. On 30 June Washington forwarded to John Jay, President of the Continental Congress, news of the resignation of Colonel Daniel Morgan from Continental service. Morgan had joined the Continental Army in 1775 and his letter of resignation cataloged his long service, pointing out that he commanded over 1,200 men during the Saratoga campaign. Morgan stated that, given his service and experience, he expected to be given command of the light corps when it was formed but noted 'I am however disappointed, such a corps has been form'd and the command of it given to another'. Morgan mentioned two officers, apparently

---

30   Robert K, Wright, *The Continental Army* (Washington, D.C.: Center of Military History, 1989), pp.455-456.

in reference to Wayne and Butler, and observed that 'I am an older officer than either of the gentlemen who have succeeded me.'[31]

---

31 Washington to Jay, 30 June 1779, *Founders Online,* National Archives.

7

The Plan to Assault Stony Point

Having received Washington's urgent summons on 21 June Wayne arrived at Washington's relocated headquarters at New Windsor as June turned into July. Washington's discussion with Wayne must have included an update on efforts to date to determine British intentions and, more importantly, Washington must have provided recent intelligence and broached the subject of a possible attack on the British forts at Kings Crossing. In his 6 June report to John Jay concerning the British capture of the Stony Point and Verplanck's Point Washington admitted Clinton's 'movements and conduct are very perplexing – and leave it difficult to determine what are their real Objects'. While Washington could not be certain that the West Point forts were not Clinton's ultimate objective he conceded that 'one part of their expedition and a principal one, is to cut off communications by the way of King's ferry by establishing garrisons'.[1]

On 11 June Washington responded to Major General Horatio Gates who had developed a wildly unrealistic plan for an assault on New York based on faulty intelligence that Clinton had severely denuded the garrison. After pointing out the error in Gates' calculations, stating that, even with the reductions that resulted from the various detachments, Clinton was obliged to make sure there were still approximately 11,000 British troops defending New York, Washington turned to the subject of the British advance up the Hudson. He granted the action was 'judicious on their part and will be productive of advantages to them and inconveniences to us' and lamented any 'attempt to dislodge them, from the natural strength of the positions, would require a greater force and apparatus than we are masters of. All we can do is lament what we cannot remedy and to endeavor to prevent further progress on the river'.[2]

Seemingly resolved to accept British control of Kings Ferry, Washington remained vigilant about the safety of West Point. At the same time he began to contemplate some attack on the British. While his various sources of intelligence could not confirm British interest in West Point, he was certain that Clinton was desperate to force the Continental Army from a position of safety and bring it to battle. By the middle of June Washington had

1   Washington to Jay, 6 June 1779, *Founders Online,* National Archives.
2   Washington to Gates, 11 June 1779, *Founders Online,* National Archives.

repositioned the main Continental Army along Smith's Clove, strengthened his garrisons at West Point, and modified his dispositions on the east bank of the Hudson and yet still the British did not appear to be moving. If anything, Clinton had pulled back troops from the King's Ferry crossing to be closer to New York, suggesting his goal was not to threaten West Point. What Washington did know was that the British were fortifying both Stony Point and Verplanck's Point with the intention to remain in possession of a key Continental communications route.

While protection of West Point remained his primary concern Washington had taken the prudent step of requesting heightened efforts to collect intelligence on the condition and nature of the enhanced fortifications at both Stony Point and Verplanck's Point. He assigned Major Henry 'Lighthorse Harry' Lee's Legion the task of monitoring the Kings Ferry dispositions of the British. Lee provided Washington with a detailed summary of the expanded works, type, and location of artillery positions, naval vessels deployed, and units assigned to Stony Point on 21 June. Lee also advised Washington that the recent British redeployments suggested a move up the East River rather than a continuation of the threat towards West Point.

On the east bank of the Hudson River Major General William Heath was responsible for gathering intelligence, monitoring British activity, and protecting supply centers at Continental Village and Peekskill. Heath's command included the Massachusetts brigade of Brigadier General John Nixon and the Connecticut brigades of Brigadier General Jedidiah Huntington and Brigadier General Samuel Parsons. Heath ordered a reconnaissance on 29 June to probe the Verplanck's Point defenses by a company of light infantry under the command of Colonel Rufus Putnam.

Always wary of British designs on West Point, despite the evidence that Clinton had pulled back the bulk of his forces to New York City, Washington passed along another warning to Heath the next day, relaying information received from Gates, that a large force of British units had been detached from the Rhode Island garrison, bound for an unknown destination. Although Clinton had in fact detached the Rhode Island units to replace those assigned to Tyron's task force assembled to raid Connecticut, Washington immediately assumed Clinton had possible designs on the Hudson Highlands.

In all probability, Washington intended to regain control over the King's Ferry from the moment Clinton captured Stony Point and Verplanks Point. Given his initial skepticism about the possibility of an assault on the forts it is unclear when he resolved to undertake the attack. Some of his thinking was reflected in his 1 July instructions to Wayne. With Wayne finally in camp to take command of the Light Infantry Corps, Washington issued him specific directions reflecting his thoughts about the effort to secure Kings Ferry. 'The importance of the two posts of Verplanks and Stoney points to the enemy is too obvious to need explanation. We ought if possible to dispossess them … It is a matter I have much at heart to make some attempt upon these Posts'. Washington directed Wayne to continue gather intelligence on British dispositions, their fortifications and the nature of the ground. A possible insight into Washington renewed interest in the attack is reflected in his suggestion that the fort garrisons had been weakened and Clinton's attention may have been diverted to other projects. Washington asked for Wayne's opinion concerning a surprise attack on one or both of the forts but 'especially that on the west side of the River'.[3]

With Washington's instructions fresh in his mind, Wayne joined the Light Corps on 2 July at Sandy Beach. Sandy Beach was located in close proximity to Fort Montgomery and allowed the Light Corps to monitor British activity between West Point and Kings Ferry. Although gratified to be back in command and assigned to lead army's elite unit, the sight that greeted Wayne must have been troubling. His men, like the army at large, suffered from persistent lack of adequate clothing and supplies. Wayne found the Light Corps dressed in a combination of blue and brown uniforms, depending on which State regiments they were from. Shoes were worn out and tents scarce. Having had to deal with bitter struggles to provision his Pennsylvania division over the last year Wayne, while disappointed, set to work. His first request was to Major General McDougal at West Point for a provision of rum, which McDougal grudgingly agreed to provide as a loan, to be repaid by Wayne. After taking stock of the condition of the Light Corps, Wayne found it lacked the basic elements necessary to operate as an independent body. He wrote somewhat despairingly to Washington on 4 July proposing to appoint a brigade quarter master to the Light Corps who would be responsible for the provision of supplies. He asked for baggage wagons and appointment of someone to be responsible for foraging. Wayne also requested copies of the *Regulations for the Order and Discipline of the Troops of the United States*, authored by Major General von Steuben, to use for training. Wayne turned his attention to the appearance of his Corps writing that if Washington was amenable Wayne believed 'we shall have it in our power to Introduce Uniformity among the Light Corps belonging to the Respective States & Infuse a Laudable pride and Emulation into the Whole – which in a Soldier is a Substitute for almost every Other Virtue'. Wayne went on to acknowledge that he had a 'prejudice in favor of an Elegant Uniform and Soldierly appearance'.[4]

Washington received updated information about the Verplanks Point defenses from Heath on 3 July. Heath provided a map prepared by Colonel Rufus Putnam, based on information gathered at Washington's direction, showing various features of the fort, including the extent of abates and the location of block houses and other fortified buildings.

While Heath collected intelligence on Verplanks Point, Major Henry Lee's Legion continued to monitor the Stony Point defenses. Although Lee's men were easily able to determine that the British had constructed an extensive set of defenses on Stony Point, Washington was interested in obtaining a more thorough picture of the fortifications. Captain Allan McLane was selected to enter the Stony Point position and gather the information. McLane and his company of Delaware light infantry were attached to Lee's force. McLane, 33, joined the Continental Army in 1775 along with his Delaware militia company and saw action over the next several years. McLane came to the attention of Washington and was utilized in a variety of roles, usually

3   Washington to Wayne, 1 July 1779, *Founders Online,* National Archives.
4   Wayne to Washington, 4 July 1779, *Founders Online,* National Archives.

operating independently. McLane undertook the mission, acting as a militia officer, accompanying a Mrs. Smith, under a flag of truce into the Stony Point fortifications. The British failed to blindfold McLane who made mental notes on the British nature of the fortifications, location and type of artillery and state of the garrison. A British officer engaged McLane in conversation, asking him 'Well Captain, what do you think of our fortress is it strong enough to keep Mister Washington out?' McLane replied innocently that he knew 'nothing of these matters' but thought 'I guess the General would be likely to think a bit, before he would run his head against such works as these'. The British officer declared 'this is the Gibraltar of America, and defended by British valour, must be deemed impregnable'. McLane replied simply 'No doubt, no doubt … as far as we are concerned you may sleep in security'.[5]

The same day as McLane entered the Stony Point works, Wayne, along with Butler and Steward, made their own reconnaissance. The next day, 3 July, Wayne summarized his impressions to Washington, concluding the Stony Point works 'in my Opinion are formidable – (I think too much so for Storm)'. He observed that the positions at Verplanks Point were no less formidable and while a direct assault on Stony Point was out of the question Wayne wondered 'but perhaps a Surprize may be Effected'.[6] In addition to a surprise attack Wayne also suggested drawing part of the garrison out of their defenses at Stony Point through a feint, ambushing them and then carrying the attack into the works. Towards that end he directed Butler on 5 July to undertake a night reconnaissance to identify locations that might be used to carry out this strategem.

Wayne invited Washington to join him on a reconnaissance so that they could discuss further options. Washington agreed to meet Wayne on 6 July and supported his efforts to find appropriate uniforms for his men but cautioned that 'it might have an ill effect to make too great a difference between the infantry and the troops of the line at large'.[7] Washington did agree to order the clothier to supply Wayne with hats, blankets, shirts, overalls, and shoes and directed the commissary to send rum. In order to ensure the Light Corps maintained effective strength Washington ordered all vacancies in the light infantry companies occasioned by death, sickness or desertion be immediately replaced from volunteers of their parent regiments.

Washington joined Wayne on 6 July and, under the protection of McLane's Delaware company, examined the Stony Point position. Between the information previously collected by Lee, McLane, and others, and their own evaluation Washington and Wayne agreed a daylight assault would be costly and probably unsuccessful. Although their activities did not draw a response from the British garrison at Stony Point a curious letter, written by a British soldier at Stony Point on 7 July, was printed on 12 July in the *New York Gazette and the Weekly Mercury*: 'Yesterday Mr. Washington, with several other Rebel Officers were reconnoitering our Post, attended with about 500 Men, 13 of which Number, chose to come in to us in the Course of

---

5   Alexander Garden, *Anecdotes of the American Revolution* (Charleston S.C.: A.E. Miller, 1828), pp.79-80.

6   Wayne to Washington, 3 July 1779,' *Founders Online,* National Archives.

7   Washington to Wayne, 5 July 1779, *Founders Online,* National Archives.

the Day, by whom we learn, That the Report among them is, That an Attack on the Post is intended. I have not a doubt that it will prove a very serious Affair to them'.[8]

Upon returning to his headquarters that evening Washington began to learn about the British incursion into Connecticut. He immediately sent notice to Connecticut Governor Jonathan Trumbull, warning him that a force estimated at 1,800 men was moving east from New York City. Washington was probably not surprised at the news of the British movement against Connecticut. From intelligence he had already received he knew the British had withdrawn units from the Kings Ferry defenses and had recently been alerted from various sources that a portion of the British Rhode Island garrison had been withdrawn. Washington also knew from his spies that Clinton had discussed the utility of a raid into Connecticut to draw Washington away from the Highlands. To Trumbull Washington suggested the British objective might be to both attack a coastal supply center and in the process cause the Continental Army to leave the Hudson Valley.

On 7 July Washington was notified by Gates that he had dispatched, at Washington's request, Brigadier General John Glover's Massachusetts Brigade from the Rhode Island garrison to take up positions at Peekskill. Seizing the opportunity to respond to the British expedition into Connecticut, Washington issued orders to Glover the next day, notifying him of the possible British attack and directing him to march near the Long Island Sound and be prepared to respond to news of a British attack and assist the Connecticut militia as necessary. That same day Washington detached Brigadier General Samuel Parsons from his brigade and directed him to proceed to Connecticut to take command of the militia, although Washington hoped this absence would be for only a short time.

Trumbull was already well aware of the British attack, writing himself to Washington on 7 July with details of Tyron's attack on New Haven. Trumbull admitted he was unsure whether the British would remain or attack another location, although he suspected the later. He informed Washington that he was aware of Brigadier General Glover's march from Rhode Island and had taken the opportunity to request his assistance.

Washington responded immediately to Trumbull approving of his request for Glover's assistance and notifying him of his detachment of Parsons. Parsons reported to Washington on 9 July detailing the British devastation of New Haven and Fairfield and postulating their next move would be against Norwalk. He reported that Connecticut militia General Oliver Wolcott passed along reports of a large British force, 4,000 strong, at Horseneck, New York, marching east into Connecticut, and although he had not yet seen Glover's troops, he believed more Continental troops would bolster the resolve of the Connecticut militia.

Parsons reported again to Washington on 10 July, providing further details of the British raids and more rumors about a British attack from Horseneck. Estimates of British strength at Horseneck had grown to 8,000 men with 12 cannon. Parsons told Washington he would ride to Horseneck to confirm the

---

8   Quoted in an editorial footnote to Washington to Jonathan Trumbull Sr., 7 July 1779, *Founders Online*, National Achieves.

information. The British identified at Horseneck were the force Clinton had dispatched to support the Connecticut raids, although he had no intention of using these troops to invade the state. Parsons closed his note by again asking Washington to detach Continental troops to Connecticut but made it clear he should do so only if West Point were secure.

In response to the news from Connecticut, Washington wrote Major General William Heath, updating him with what he knew about British movements, including the possibility of an attack from Horseneck. He directed Heath to march the next morning, 11 July, with both his brigades, to assist the Connecticut militia in defending against the British raids. Washington cautioned Heath that these raids might be a diversion to mask an attack on West Point, and that he should maintain regular communications with the main army to ensure he could respond as necessary. He ordered Heath to work with Brigadier General Parsons to coordinate militia actions and placed Glover, whose brigade was expected to arrive in Connecticut shortly, under his command.

The British attack on Connecticut complicated Washington's thinking about an attack on the Kings Ferry forts. While he knew Clinton's strike at Connecticut was largely intended to force him to respond in a manner that would put the Continental Army at risk, at the same time the disruption of the fall harvest caused by the raids threatened a major source of food on which his army depended. He also understood the deprivations against Fairfield and Norwalk further depressed public support for the Continental cause, which, after four years of war, was flagging. Further loss of public support would have a negative impact on future Continental recruitment and the response of state militias to British attacks.

It was with some hesitancy that Washington detached three Continental brigades in response to the British invasion. While these detachments weakened his ability to resist a British advance north from Kings Ferry, Washington knew from information about recent troop re-dispositions that Clinton did not have enough resources to simultaneously attack Connecticut, protect New York, and threaten West Point. With Clinton's attention focused elsewhere Washington immediately understood the time was ripe for an attempt on Stony Point and Verplank's Point. Not only did conditions appear favorable for success, but a victory could restore any loss of public support lost by the British successes in Connecticut.

Washington reflected his understanding of the implications of the Connecticut raids in a 9 July note to Wayne, 'while the enemy are making incursions to distress the country it has a very disagreeable aspect to remain in a state of inactivity on our part. The reputation of the army and the good of the service seem to exact some attempt from it. The importance of Stoney Point to the enemy makes it infinitely desirable that could be the object'.[9]

Having established that an attempt should be made soon and Stony Point should be the target, Washington turned his attention to practical issues. He thought that while the works appeared formidable they appeared to have a weakness. He passed along to Wayne information from a British deserter identifying a sandy beach along the southern approach to the fort, along

---

9   Washington to Wayne, 9 July 1779, *Founders Online,* National Archives.

the Hudson River. The deserter claimed that the abatis was not extensive in this area and access to the fort might be achieved by this route. Washington directed Wayne to gather as much information as possible and provide him with a plan based on the concept of a night-time surprise attack.

Wayne's concerns on 9 July were more practical. Although the light companies that made up the Light Corps were all from the same Continental Army and many of the senior officers were familiar with each other, the privates and non-commissioned officers who composed the bulk of the companies came from different brigades and divisions of the army, in fact from different states of the colonies, and had never trained or operated together. Wayne understood the value of establishing a sense of familiarity, reliability, and comradery between units that were shortly to be ordered to operate in the most difficult of conditions, fighting over rugged terrain that was wholly unknown to them, at night, and against fortifications that were only partially identified. Wayne's wish was 'to draw the Light Corps together in order to Manoeuvre them & to give the Officers and men an Opportunity to mix and become acquainted with each Other – as also to Introduce a Similarity of dress and duty'.[10] Wayne also reported that he had assigned a small detachment of riflemen to harass the garrison at Stony Point with the intent to keep the defenders on edge and possibly encourage additional desertions.

In addition to hoping to regularize uniforms, Wayne also focused on his men's weapons and found them wanting. In particular he appeared particularly concerned about the officers. Perhaps the recent memory of his officers trying to defend themselves in vain during the panic and confusion of the night at Paoli in a fight against British troops light infantry brandishing 18 inch bayonets caused him to write Washington. 'Your Excellency must have Observed how wretched our Officers were armed – many of them without any – of Consequence should they ever come to a Charge in place of producing an example of fortitude to their men they must Inevitably be the first to give'.[11] In consequence Wayne requested his officers be provided with Espontoons. Espontoons or spontoons were staffs five or six feet in length, topped with a blade. The use of spontoons began in the 17th century, being used by officers to defend themselves in close combat. They were also used to align the infantry lines during combat. Although usually assigned to officers, Washington had in the past proposed issuing spontoons to riflemen. The riflemen, armed with long rifles without bayonets, were vulnerable to attack by enemy infantry armed with bayonets, particularly during the time it took to reload the rifle. Wayne's concern was heightened by the prospect of the imminent assault on Stony Point and he proposed to undertake to train his officers in the use of the weapon over the next several days.

After reviewing the collective intelligence, and several discussions with Wayne, Washington prepared a lengthy outline for the attack on Stony Point. Washington proposed the attack should be attempted at night, with an advance force of 200 chosen light infantry approaching the fort along the beach in order to circumvent the abatis. A smaller detachment should proceed ahead

---

10   Wayne to Washington, 9 July 1779, *Founders Online,* National Archives.
11   Wayne to Washington, 10 July 1779, *Founders Online,* National Archives.

of this group to remove obstructions and eliminate any sentries. The entire force should attack with fixed bayonets and unloaded muskets. Each officer should be assigned a specific objective to avoid confusion once they gained entry to the fortifications.

The main body of the light infantry should follow the advance party at a short distance and move into the fort by several different routes. Each member of the light infantry should wear a white feather or badge on their hat to identify them in the darkness. If successful in breaking into the fort, Washington directed that Wayne should cut off any attempt by the garrison to escape by water and that the British guns, once captured, should immediately be used to bombard Verplank's Point. Washington cautioned that secrecy was essential to success and the defection of a single deserter would compromise the entire enterprise. Washington recommended that information about the attack's objective should be withheld until the last moment and officers should be vigilant to prevent any loss of secrecy. He also recommended midnight, preferably on a rainy night, as the time for the attack and suggested that a company of artillerymen should accompany Wayne to man the British artillery once the fort was captured. Washington cautioned that his recommendations were only that, and Wayne had large leeway to modify any element of the plan as he saw fit.

Washington closed by agreeing to send Wayne the spontoons requested and buttressed his force by assigning additional light infantry to supplement Wayne's initial two-regiment formation. In ordering Heath's Connecticut division to march to Connecticut, Washington had stipulated that the light infantry companies be left behind. From Heath's brigades eight companies of light infantry, totaling 300 men under the command Lieutenant Colonel Return Jonathan Meigs, made up Wayne's 3rd Regiment. At age 39, commander of the 6th Connecticut Meigs was a veteran who had joined the Connecticut militia in 1775. After deployment with Washington's army at Boston, Meigs' unit accompanied the army in the Canadian invasion. Like his compatriot Christian Febiger, Meigs was captured during the unsuccessful assault on Quebec and paroled in 1777.

Commanding the 1st Battalion of Meigs Regiment was Lieutenant Colonel Isaac Sherman, 26. Sherman joined Washington's army in 1776 and endured the reverses at Long Island and New York before retreating with the army through New Jersey. By 1779 Sherman commanded the 2nd Connecticut. The 2nd Battalion, of four companies like the 1st, was led by Lieutenant Colonel Henry Champion. Champion, 28, joined the Continental Army in 1775, fought at Bunker Hill and was commissioned in 1777 as captain in 3rd Connecticut Regiment.

The 4th Light Infantry Regiment was a mixed force of 350 men, composed of six companies from Massachusetts regiments and two from North Carolina. Its commander, Major William Hull, 26, also commanded the 1st Battalion of four companies. As a member of the 7th Provisional Connecticut, or Webb's Regiment, Captain Hull fought at New York and White Plains and was promoted to major for his actions at Trenton in 1776. Hull helped recruit the 8th Connecticut and as part of that unit participated in the Saratoga and Monmouth campaigns. The 2nd Battalion was led by North Carolina Major

Hardy Murfree. Murfree, 27, was commissioned a captain in the 2nd North Carolina Regiment in 1775. Promoted to major in 1777, Murfree fought with the main army at Monmouth in 1778.

On 12 July Washington asked Major Henry Lee to maintain a close watch on British movements along the Hudson River and alert him immediately if there was evidence of an enemy movement. He also responded to Connecticut Governor Jonathan Trumbull, confirming that he had dispatched Major General Heath's division to assist the militia in resisting the British invasion. He expressed regret that he could not send more resources, reminding Trumbull about the importance of the Hudson forts and that control of the waterways allowed the British could to strike at will.

Over the next two days Wayne and Washington focused on the details of the attack on Stony Point. Although he had given up pursuing a coordinated attack against Stony Point and Verplank's Point, Washington ordered Colonel Rufus Putnam undertake a diversion against Verplank's Point while Wayne was attacking Stony Point. With that in mind he ordered Major General Alexander McDougall to march Nixon's brigade south to Continental Village on 14 July. From there Putnam was expected to take as many men as needed to Verplank's Point during the evening of 15 July to support Wayne's attack. Due to his concerns about secrecy, Washington only told Putnam of his plan for Wayne to attack Stony Point and forbade him to tell any others. This placed Putnam in a difficult situation when, on 14 July, he discovered that Nixon's brigade had not marched as expected, but that McDougall had agreed to delay the movement and in any case Nixon only planned on sending 50 men. With the knowledge that Wayne would attack at midnight on 15 July but unable to reveal that information, Putnam told McDougall and Nixon simply that he was under special orders from Washington, that he needed at least 100 men, and that they should march first thing the morning of 15 July.

On 14 July Washington directed Wayne to assault Stony Point the next day, 15 July. Wayne acknowledged the order and promised to provide Washington with his proposed disposition of his troops and a detailed plan on 15 July. The stage was set for the attack on Stony Point.

8

American Attack

Wayne sent Washington his plan for attack on Stony Point on 15 July at 11:00 am. Wayne noted that he and Colonel Butler had conducted a final reconnaissance of Stony Point several days before, and he suggested he that had discussed his plan with his senior officers, who supported his proposal. Wayne proposed to split his force into three columns. Two columns would assault the British works and force their way into the fort, while the third column demonstrated as a feint to draw British attention from the points of the main attacks.

Wayne stipulated that the Light Infantry would march with the right column was led by Febiger's regiment, formed into half platoons, followed by Colonel Meigs and Major Hull's regiments. Colonel Butler was ordered to form his men into a column to the left of Febiger's regiment. All men were directed to place a piece of white paper in their hats to help distinguish them during the confusion of the melee in the darkness.

At the head of the right column Colonel Fleury was assigned 150 men to form the advance company who were to go forward with unloaded muskets. Preceding Fleury's men was a small 'forlorn hope' of 20 men, commanded by Lieutenant George Knox, whose task it was to overwhelm the sentries and remove the abatis to allow the men following to charge in to the fort. Wayne would accompany Febiger with this column. Once the Americans had penetrated the fortifications Wayne directed his men to shout repeatedly in a loud voice, 'the fort's our own'.[1]

Colonel Butler's column, which was also to be led by an advance company of 100 men under the leadership of Major John Steward, was ordered to attack the fort on the left. A forlorn hope of 20 men, led by Lieutenant James Gibbons, was to be detached from the advance company to remove the obstacles and overpower the sentries. These men were also ordered to shout the watch phrase once they had entered the works. Major Murfree's two companies of North Carolina light infantry, part of the 2nd Battalion of Major Hull's 4th Regiment, would march with Butler's column but separate as they approached the fort and take position in the middle of the British line, at the causeway that crossed the swamp. From that position Murfree's men

---

1   Henry Dawson, *The Assault on Stony Point by General Anthony Wayne, Gleanings from the Harvest of American History* (New York: Morrisania, 1863), p.37.

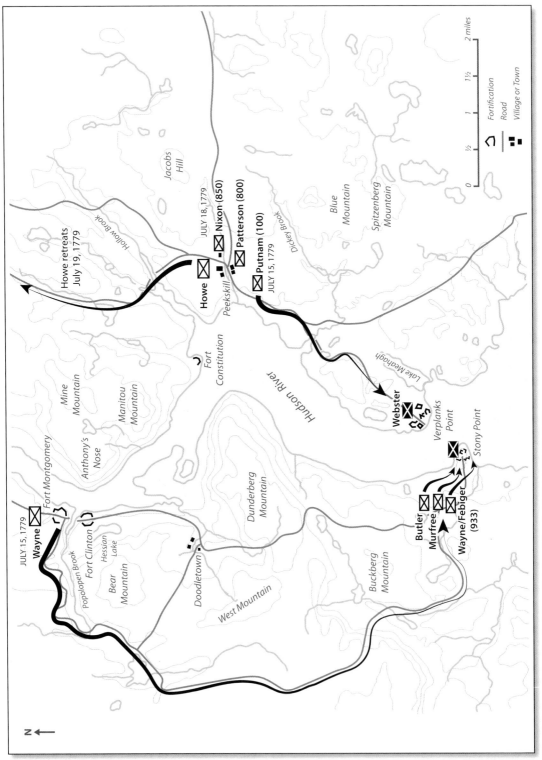

The American advance Against Stony Point and Verplank's Point, 15 July 1779.

were ordered to keep up 'a perpetual and Gauling fire & endeavor to enter between and possess the works'.[2]

Wayne issued a stern warning to all his men. In order to guarantee complete surprise soldiers were ordered to keep their muskets shouldered at all times and if anyone appeared ready to fire or advance against the enemy without orders officers were ordered to immediately put that man to death. The troops were ordered to maintain complete silence during their approach to the British positions. Wayne reminded the men it was an honor to have been chosen for the Light Infantry Corps and the reputations of their parent regiments and their respective States was at stake.

Recognizing that reliance on personal merit alone might not be enough motivation to risk the dangers of a night assault on prepared works, Wayne offered a 500 dollar reward to the first man entering the works. The next four men after him would also receive a cash reward.

On the morning of 15 July Wayne's force was completed by the arrival of Hull's men and the artillerists assigned by Washington. At around noon, Wayne held a review of his troops on Sandy Beach. Once completed, rather than being dismissed, the men were directed to begin their march south. As one, 1,300 men moved past the ruins of Fort Montgomery into the Hell Hole, a gap between Bear Mountain and the Torne. The men must have sensed the seriousness of their march when the column took the southwestern fork, marching past the Doodletown trail and finally stopping to refresh themselves behind West Mountain. They then marched along the ridge connecting West and Black Mountains. Somewhere beyond that point they were joined by Henry Lee's Legion who led them through a maze of forest trails along the final stretch to a point one and a half miles west of Stony Point. After marching approximately 10 miles, the men rested at nightfall, still uncertain of their ultimate objective. The Light Corps settled down at the David Springsteel Farm and waited. In order to protect against a warning given by local residents, Wayne dispatched small groups of light infantry to position themselves along the three approaches to the fort and cut off all communication between the fort and the outside region

After a final quick look at Stony Point, which appeared completely unware of the impending attack, Wayne met briefly with Captain Allan McLane and Henry Lee. During the evening a strong wind from the north shook the trees and helped mask the sounds of Wayne's force as it prepared to march. McLane and Lee reported the wind had also caused the British ships, the *Cornwallis* and *Vulture*, to move away from Stony Point and take up positions nearer to Verplank's Point. The movement of the ships and loss of their supporting fire was good fortune, particularly for Febiger's southern column which would move slowly through the shallow water of the Hudson shore, all the while exposed to fire from the galley. With this information Wayne returned to the Springsteel Farm and wrote a letter to his brother-in-law, Sharp Delaney.

In the letter he told Delaney he expected to die in the coming assault and asked him to look after his wife and family. It is impossible to know if Wayne's pessimism was simple dramatics or whether he believed there was a good chance he would not survive the attack. He did believe his men had a

---

2   Quoted in Dawson, *Assault on Stony Point*, p.37.

reasonable chance of success if they could surprise the British and overwhelm them before they recovered from their initial shock. He knew from personal experience the great advantage attacking troops would have in the darkness to dispatch their enemies in a most brutal manner with the bayonet, and how fear and confusion could paralyze both soldiers and officers. He probably also understood that, given the restricted ability of the British defenders to retreat or run away, an option his men at Paoli used to their benefit to escape their attackers, the bulk of the British defenders would be trapped within the fortifications and would sell their lives dearly. While the Americans would capture the fort, the cost would be high on both sides. He knew the British cannon, if brought into action and used effectively, could inflict huge casualties and break his men's momentum, which was key to victory.

Based on his knowledge of the layout of the position, Wayne had assigned each of the officers a specific objective after they gained entry to the fort. These objectives, probably in the form of easily identified objects such as the fleches, batteries, or flagpole, were key to victory. In the dark and confusion it was anyone's guess as to whether the officers and their men would be able to move quickly to their objectives or become confused and disoriented, allowing the British to organize themselves to defend the fort. If the Americans momentum did not carry them past the upper abatis and into the Upper Works there was every possibility the attack would bog down and British firepower would decimate the American light infantry milling around the Lower Works in search of a way to breach the Upper Works. In that case Wayne would have to order a costly assault with very little chance of success, or else withdraw. Neither was a palatable option.

His letter finished Wayne and his officers addressed their men at 11:00 pm, telling them of the plan to attack Stony Point, outlining the need for strict silence, on pain of death, and offering the reward for the first five men that entered the British works. Any man unwilling to undertake the mission, which he admitted would be dangerous, could drop out of the ranks. In the pitch darkness of a moonless night white paper was distributed, bayonets fixed to muskets, and at 11:15 pm the columns began their final march to Stony Point.

Wayne accompanied the south or right column, led by plan Colonel Febiger. Wayne's plan designated Febiger's force as the main attack column. Butler's left or north column would attack a more formidable set of defenses, but Wayne was counting on Murfree's diversion and the success of Febiger's column to give Butler's men a chance to break in to the fort. In turn the success of Febiger's assault hinged on their ability to move rapidly through the first line of abatis and move swiftly through the British works before the defenders could react in any strength. Wayne and Washington believed the southern approach had the best chance of entering the British defenses using the shallow beach along the Hudson River shore to get around the abatis.

Both columns approached their jump-off positions on the edge of the swamp about midnight. Butler's column moved left while Wayne and Febiger moved to the right. Murfree's North Carolina troops advanced towards the causeway and everyone waited. Wayne delayed his order to advance about 20 minutes to allow the tide to subside.

Although Wayne and his officers were unaware of it, the British were not completely unsuspecting. Several days before the attack several American deserters entered Stony Point and reported to Lieutenant Colonel Johnson that the Americans were planning for an attack. Johnson brought together his subordinates and staff, passed along the information, and coordinated a response in the event of an attack. The number and location of pickets to be deployed each evening was clarified. Johnson ordered

Hillside terrain crossed by Continental attack columns at Stony Point (Author's photo).

four companies of the 17th Foot and the two 71st Highland grenadier companies to immediately occupy positions along the Lower Works abatis. The remaining four companies of the 17th, joined by the Loyal American company, were ordered to occupy the Upper Works. The artillery was to man their guns in the Lower and Upper Works.

Due to continuing concerns about a possible attack Johnson refused to implement a sign and countersign system for fear the Americans might discover the countersign and surprise the garrison. On the evening of 15 July two more American deserters arrived at Stony Point with information about an imminent attack. As a consequence Johnson issued an order requiring his men 'to Lay with all their Cloaths on at Night, Except Coats which with their Arms, Ammunition and Accoutrements is to be Carefully put up in such a manner as they can get them upon the Shortest Notice'.[3] From the information provided by the two deserters and his own scouts although Johnson believed an attack was to be expected he also believed the Americans were planning on deploying heavy artillery to support the attack, which suggested no imminent threat.

Johnson established six pickets some distance outside the Lower Works. A total of 88 men and officers were assigned to the posts, with instructions to respond to an enemy advance by firing a warning shot and then retiring into the Lower Works. As part of the detachment Lieutenant John Ross of the 71st Highland Grenadiers was posted with 30 men near the bridge over the marsh.

While the row galley *Cornwallis* had withdrawn from its station off the southern shore due to the high winds the garrison was used to the ship being off station. For a variety of reasons on several occasions in the past the *Cornwallis* had been moved away from its usual station, which was close enough to shore that the picket could hear its bell and shout out to the ship. On the night of 15 July the southernmost picket of nine men heard nothing

---

3   Quoted in Loprieno, *The Enterprise in Contemplation*, p.143.

THE BATTLE OF STONY POINT.

Stylized engraving of Continental assault at Stony Point, by Alonzo Chappel, 1857(Library of Congress).

from the ship and assumed the strong wind masked the usual sounds. The absence of contact with the *Cornwallis* did not appear to cause concern among the picket or the officers. Due to the high winds the *Vulture* was also off station, taking position due east of the point, where she could provide no support to either flank.

After waiting until approximately 00:20 the American columns began to move. On the north Colonel Butler pushed forward gingerly in the darkness, while on the south Colonel Febiger along with Brigadier General Wayne splashed into the marsh and towards the shallow bank of Havershaw Bay. Major Murfree marched his two companies forward and they were the first to engage the enemy as they advanced east towards the causeway over the marsh. At the sound of musket fire to his front, Lieutenant John Ross of the 71st Highlanders, commanding 30 men deployed outside the Lower Works, dispatched several men to investigate. They returned immediately with the sentry who had fired the shot. They all agreed that the Americans were somewhere in the darkness. When a second sentry fired at the hidden movement Ross ordered his drummer to beat the call to arms. Although alert to the possible danger, Ross was initially unsure if he should retire into the Lower Works. While he was discussing the best course of action with another officer, the night was rent by the rattle of a volley of musket fire from the main body of British troops in the Upper Works. Ross immediately collected his men and retired to the Lower Works. After passing through the abatis Ross was knocked down by a soldier in darkness. He assumed a jittery soldier had mistaken him for the enemy. He only discovered later that he had been confronted by American light infantry that had infiltrated the Lower Works. More scattered musket fire from the area near the Upper Works added to the growing confusion.

Murfree's men began firing as they advanced, creating the impression of a general attack being launched across the causeway towards to center of the British lines. The impact of their diversionary fire had the result Washington and Wayne had hoped for. British attention was drawn, even if momentarily, to the center and away from the main American thrusts along both flanks. Corporal Simon Davies of the 17th Foot commanded the 15-man picket nearest the southern shore. Davies deployed a body of six men 100 yards in advance of the creek while he remained with nine near the shoreline, between the creek and Upper Works. Davies was surprised by the initial exchange of musket fire to his right and ordered his men to be alert. Davies then heard his men deployed beyond the creek open fire at the same time as a second round of firing echoed from his right. Now thoroughly alarmed, Davies moved forward intending to check on his advanced sentries, but met them as they retired towards his position.

After collecting his men and beginning to retire Davies observed 'a Noise in the Water on my left, which appeared to me to have been Occasioned by a large body of Men wading through it'.[4] Davies also heard American officers ordering their men not to fire and keep quiet. Davies and his men quickly retreated to the Lower Works near Fleche #1. He deployed his men on either side of the 12lb gun deployed there, ordering his men to fire down towards the shoreline and towards the marsh. Lieutenant William Horndon commanded the cannon and 'began firing the 12 Pdr. to a particular Object, to which I was Order'd to point that Gun, in case of an Alarm'. The 12lb gun was sighted towards the marsh causeway, unable to turn to fire towards the river shoreline. Horndon shifted the cannon as best he could left and right to try and cover as much of the approach from the marsh as possible, although he noted 'by the light occasioned by the flash of the Gun I could perceive a Body of them coming thro' the Water; upon the left'.[5] Thinking he might need additional ammunition Horndon dispatched two men to the magazine, located in the Upper Works and continued firing ineffectively into the marsh. The men at Fleche #1, now totaling 31, were unaware that the Americans and the struggle for Stony Point had moved past them.

At the other end of the Lower Works defensive line, along the north shore of the Hudson, Corporal John Ash had split his 15-man piquet, sending 6 men to stand guard outside the Lower Works abatis, near Fleche #3, while he took station with the remainder about a quarter of a mile away from the abatis, near the ferry landing. After hearing the first sounds of musket fire from the causeway area, Ash recalled his men and, with the firing intensifying, he tried to lead them along the shoreline to enter the Lower Works at the end of the abatis. As he moved towards the line of abatis he discovered that a column of Americans extended from the ferry landing towards the abatis, cutting him and his men off. At the same time the Highland Grenadiers posted along the Lower Works abatis poured a steady fire towards the Americans, wounding

---

4   Quoted in Loprieno, *The Enterprise in Contemplation*, p.228.
5   Quoted in Loprieno, *The Enterprise in Contemplation*, p.176.

Continental assault at Stony Point, by Alonzo Chappel 1857 (Library of Congress).

one of Ash's men. Ash ordered his men to take cover and keep out of sight.

Along the southern shore the American column struggled through the shallow water of the Bay, described by Major Hull as two feet in depth. Although it was summer, the cold water of the Bay, coupled with the strong north wind, chilled the men. While the men were admonished to remain quiet the movement of nearly 700 men through the water was accompanied by the noise of splashing and cursing as the men made their way past the outer edge of the Lower Works abatis, under the eyes of the British pickets. The main group, commanded by Febiger, totaled approximately 550 men. Preceding Febiger's group was Lieutenant Colonel de Fleury's 130-man vanguard, including Major Posey, which followed closely behind the forlorn hope. This group of 20 volunteers, led by Lieutenant George Knox, were to clear a path through the British defenses and allow de Fleury's vanguard to establish a foothold within the British works. Following behind, the main body was expected to push through de Fleury's men and fan out through the British camp. As the tip of the American spear, Knox's men understood they would be the target of British cannon and musket fire and few of them expected to survive. As the firing from the causeway area became widespread the British Lower Works erupted with a combination of musket fire from troops deployed along the abatis and cannon in the fleches. The sheets of fire briefly illuminated the landscape, exposing brief glimpses of the enemy before they were again swallowed up by the darkness. With each volley the enemy appeared closer and closer. Adding to the confusion the wind continued to howl across the hilltop distorting the noise, masking some sounds and amplifying others. While the British piquets that had discovered their movement scurried back up the hill towards the Lower Works abatis, Wayne and his men picked up their pace. Protected from cannon-fire from Fleche #1, and largely unseen by the British lining the abatis, Wayne's men suffered few casualties as they surged forward.

Once past the Lower Works abatis, Knox led his men and the following column up the steep hillside towards the Upper Works abatis. Above them and to their left they could see the flashes of fire from the British positions. They could hear the yelling of officers and men as they sought to understand their situation. In addition to the voices and echoes of muskets, punctuated by the roar of cannon, drums beat a steady tattoo calling men to arms and their stations. As Knox's men advanced into the abatis, furiously hacking and cutting, they found themselves the target of the British in the Upper Works. Although their fire proved largely ineffective in the darkness, the sheer volume of fire left several of the attackers dead or seriously wounded. In the advance up the hillside an officer of Major Hull's battalion noticed one of his men fell out of the column and stopped to load his musket. The officer reminded him of the order not to fire and ordered him back into formation. The man refused, saying 'he did not understand fighting without firing'. The officer immediately killed him, as ordered.[6]

Impatient at the pace of clearing a path through the abatis, de Fluery ordered the men of the advance guard forward to help Knox's men. Major Posey responded by leading his men forward and joining with de Fleury in directing the attack on the abatis. Responding to the unexpected delay as he had at Paoli, Wayne moved forward to the abatis to encourage his men. It was here that Wayne's forehead was grazed by a British musket ball, leaving a two inch cut, which bled profusely. Apparently armed with a spontoon, Wayne 'continued to direct it even after I had Rec'd my wound – & that at the point of my Spear– I at least helpt to direct the greater part of the Column over the Abbatis.'[7] Attended to by two aides Wayne watched for several anxious minutes while a path was hewn through the barrier and the Americans poured into the British positions. Ahead of them lay the core of the British defense.

On the northern shore Colonel Butler's attack column, although smaller, was organized in much the same manner as Febiger's. Leading the attack was a forlorn hope of 20 men, led by Lieutenant James Gibbon. Gibbon led the group by virtue of drawing lots with two other officers who requested the assignment. Following Gibbon command was the vanguard of 100 men, commanded by Major Jack Steward. The main body of 200 men was led by Lieutenant Colonel Samuel Hay. Moving silently along the dry ground above the shoreline they passed the ferry landing and entered the abatis. This section of the Lower Works abatis was defended by the two companies of the 71st Highlanders, supported by the 3lb gun deployed between the Lower and Upper Works. Captain Robert Campbell, commanding the two companies of the 71st, accompanied his men as they deployed along the right of the Lower Works abatis. During the course of the firefight Campbell was wounded in both legs and retired towards the Upper Works in search of medical attention.

A group of Butler's men appear to have pulled apart the outer abatis and entered the Lower Works near Fleche #3. Although Fleche #3 was defended by two mortars and a 12lb cannon, there is no record of any of the guns in this battery firing during the battle. Not so the 3lb cannon deployed some distance from the Lower Works. Various witnesses estimated the gun fired approximately over 69 rounds against the American attackers. This gun, along with the Highland defenders, kept up a steady fire against Gibbon's forlorn hope and Steward's supporting column as they struggled through the abatis. Taking advantage of the thin nature of the abatis in this area the Americans broke through the Lower section and headed towards the Upper Works or fanned out into the Lower Works.

In the center Murfree's men performed as ordered, firing volley after volley against the British lining the abatis at Fleche #2 and holding their attention while Butler's and Febiger's columns worked their way around the

---

6   Maria Campbell, *Revolutionary Services and Civil Life of General William Hull* (New York: D. Appleton, 1848), p.164

7   Quoted in Dawson, *Assault on Stony Point*, p.140.

Recreation of the British encampment on the top of Stony Point (Author's photo).

flanks. At the sounds of the first musket fire, Lieutenant Colonel Johnson was alert to the threat and made his way towards to Lower Works. He stopped briefly to give orders to Captain Robert Clayton who commanded the 177 men in the Upper Works. Johnson ordered Clayton to dispatch 20 men to occupy the ground between the battery on the right and the northern shoreline. He ordered Clayton to send another 12 men to the left to occupy a small infantry fleche that faced Haverstraw Bay. The remainder of Clayton's men were to defend the fortifications around the flagpole and the batteries.

With the dispositions in the Upper Works arranged Johnson moved quickly to the Lower Works, where he ordered the men defending the abatis to cease fire to allow the pickets to return to the main line. Lieutenant William Simpson, assigned to Captain Francis Tew's company, took his place with the company along the abatis near the 3lb gun. After about 10 minutes Simpson heard sounds from a large group of men off to the right and rear of his position. Assuming they were British soldiers Simpson approached them, only to be wounded and taken prisoner. Soon afterwards Lieutenant Colonel Johnson also approached the group and tried to issue them orders. They replied by attempting to bayonet Johnson, who narrowly escaped. Although they had penetrated the Lower Works the Americans appeared confused, subject to fire from several directions. The Americans left Simpson, who surrendered the next morning, and retired into the darkness.

As the pickets filtered in and took their places the British resumed firing at Murfree's men to their front and Butler's column attempting to penetrate the abatis on the right. Soon afterwards Johnson and others heard firing from the Upper Works. Captain Francis Tew directed Lieutenant Patrick Cumming to take three men to investigate the firing. Almost immediately Tew received orders from Johnson to collect as many men as possible and move back to the Upper Works. After his encounter with an unknown number of Americans between to Upper and Lower Works, and hearing the musket fire to his rear, Johnson now feared the Americans were threatening the Upper Works and was prepared to abandon the Lower Works.

Tew gathered 16 men from the grenadier companies and started up towards the Upper Works. On their way they met one of the three men who had accompanied Lieutenant Cumming. He reported that his companions had been killed and the Americans occupied the Upper Works. Avoiding a group of Americans at the main entry point Tew and his group entered the Upper Works and were immediately confronted by the enemy, who demanded their surrender. Tew apparently 'made use of some hasty expression' and was killed.[8] Lieutenant John Ross of the 71st Highlanders was part of this group and in the confusion escaped and found Lieutenant Colonel Johnson. From his observations moving from the Lower to the Upper Works Ross concluded that 'all was over'.[9]

In the Upper Works, after receiving orders from Lieutenant Colonel Johnson. Captain Clayton directed Lieutenant William Armstrong to deploy his company along the right of the Upper Works abatis, in the area that Colonel Butler's column was expected to push into the Upper Works. After deploying his men Armstrong noted the heavy fire from his left, in the area of the 3lb cannon and along the Upper and Lower Works. Seeing no threat to his immediate front Armstrong, on his own initiative, redeployed his men to his left, in the Upper Works, to protect the opening in the abatis. Armstrong positioned his men along the parapet section and although the intense noise suggested the enemy was near he could see little in the inky blackness. Perceiving the enemy to be approaching the abatis, Armstrong ordered his men to fire but after six rounds Armstrong somehow made out Lieutenant Colonel Johnson attempting to rally his men in the Lower Works. Armstrong ordered his men to cease fire and at the same time was told that the Americans had penetrated the rear of the position. Two Americans, with white paper in their hats, wandered towards Armstrong. Armstrong ordered the Americans bayoneted and after ordering the company to face to the rear and fire he was wounded in the head by a musket ball.

At Fleche #1 Lieutenant Horndon was still directing fire from 12lb gun towards the marsh and river shoreline, along with Corporal Davies' men who had been joined by a picket under the command of Corporal William West, when they heard loud cheering from the Upper Works. They also began to receive scattered fire from the direction of the Upper Works. Concerned that the two men he had dispatched for ammunition had not returned, Horndon ordered several men from the 17th and 71st to move towards Fleche #2, and a sergeant from the 17th to go to the Upper Works. The sergeant was killed and the Highlanders returned to report the Americans held most of the Lower Works. Now convinced the Americans had captured the Upper Works, and recognizing there was no escape towards the ferry, Horndon asked the men if they should turn the cannon towards the Upper Works and continue their resistance, or negotiate an honorable surrender. Finding their position untenable the men opted for surrender and Horndon approached the Upper Works, surrendering to Lieutenant Colonel Fleury.

During the time Butler's men were engaged with primarily the grenadiers of the 71st their commander, Captain Robert Campbell, who was wounded, had time to move towards the Upper Works. He was met by men from the garrison fleeing the Upper Works, telling him the Americans had taken the position. He returned briefly to Lower Works, which was also in considerable

8   Quoted in Dawson, *Assault on Stony Point*, p.164.
9   Quoted in Dawson, *Assault on Stony Point*, p.164.

confusion, before making his way to the ferry landing where he was put on a small boat and crossed to Verplank's Point.

Although the British strength in the Upper Works was impressive, featuring two batteries composed of a 24lb and 18lb cannon, two 12lb guns and two mortars, none of these guns fired in defense of their position on the night of the attack. The 24lb and 18lb guns were intended for long-range fire and ammunition was not provided for them during the night. It is unclear why the 12lb guns and mortars remained silent. In the darkness and confusion it would have been difficult to identify a target for the 12lb guns and as the Americans infiltrated into the position firing the cannon would have resulted in British troops being killed.

More troubling was the in inactivity of the mortars. Captain Clayton, ostensibly in command of the Upper Works, admitted latter that he did not order the 8-inch mortar, located just outside the Upper Works parapet, to fire and did not know who commanded the gun. Clayton approached Lieutenant John Roberts, who was in command of the artillery in the Upper Works, soon after the initial fire began at the Lower Works. In response to the firing at the Lower Works Roberts ordered the crews to their guns and then visited each battery. Finding Lieutenant Roberts at the 24lb gun in the left battery, Captain Clayton implored him to explain why the artillery was not firing. Roberts told him the ammunition was not available for these guns since they were not intended to repel an attack. After going back to check on the other battery and conferring briefly with Captain Tiffin. Roberts decided to take post with the 8-inch mortar, which he believed could do damage to the Americans crawling up the hillside, but as he approached he found the gun already captured. It is unclear why Captain Clayton did not press Lieutenant Roberts to order the 8-inch mortar to fire when they first met after the initial alarm. Roberts later testified he did not consider the mortar, which was located adjacent to the Upper Works, part of his responsibility, suggesting that it was assigned to the Lower Works artillery commander.

Captain William Tiffen was overall commander of the British artillery on 15 July, having just taken over from Captain Traille earlier that morning. Although he lacked specific orders from Lieutenant Colonel Johnson, Tiffen knew each gun, outside of the Upper Works, was to be loaded every night and positioned to fire on a predetermined target. Tiffen was aware that the 8-inch mortar had ammunition available and was oriented to fire towards Haverstraw Bay. Tiffen was also unsure who was in charge of the 8-inch mortar and, having received no orders from Lieutenant Colonel Johnson or anyone else, he did not see fit to have the mortar fired, although he was of the opinion that it would have done great damage to the Americans struggling up from Haverstraw Bay. The mortar had both case shot and solid shot available and, being able to fire one round per minute, could have had a devastating impact on Fluery's men as they reached the top of the hillside and gathered to remove the abatis.

Corporal Joseph Newton and his 12 man detachment from the 17th Foot were assigned to the mortar battery and took their positions sometime after nightfall. Newton confirmed that soon after the general alarm was given he was joined by 'Bombardier Swain … with a party of the Artillery'.[10] Newton and the artillerymen, who seemed confused and unprepared to man the mortar, noted the approach of Febinger's men making their way around the outer abatis and up the hillside. While Newton ordered his men to fire at the enemy the artillery crew remarked 'they wished that the Officer of the Artillery that commanded the Gun that Night would come and give them Orders to fire'.[11] Rather than take the initiative to engage the advancing enemy, the artillerymen retreated to the flagstaff. Newton's men defended their position for several minutes. When the American light infantry breached the abatis and began to move around the left of Newton's position, filtering into his rear, he ordered his men to turn, charge the Americans and retreat into the fortifications around the flag pole. No sooner had he given the order than his men were engaged by the American light infantry. Newton received two slight bayonet wounds before being knocked unconscious and captured.

Febiger's men penetrated the Upper Works abatis at several points. Some of the light infantry moved left, along the abatis, and pressed their way through the narrow entrance, closer to the flagpole, and over the parapet. The main body, led by Lieutenant Colonel Fluery and Major Posey, breached the Upper Works abatis just south of the 8-inch mortar emplacement, followed closely by Major Meigs, and quickly fanned out around the back of the British position. Meigs' and Hull's men passed across the front of the howitzer and infantry fleche before Meigs directed his men left, into the fortifications through the gaps in the parapet, where they overwhelmed the battery and fleche from the rear. Hull moved his men further around the back of the Upper Works and occupied the portion facing Verplank's Point, which included the 12lb gun and mortar in the unfinished battery. It was in this area that Fluery encountered Lieutenant Colonel Johnson, taking him prisoner.

The gaps in the parapets allowed the American light infantry, aided by the darkness, to move quickly to surround the British troops milling in confusion or lining the parapet facing the Lower Works. Once inside the British defenses 'the men made free use of the bayonet, and in every direction was heard, "The fort's our own"'. Lieutenant Colonel Fluery was first over the parapet and into the Upper Works, followed by Major Posey who began the cry that reverberated throughout the night, carried by the wind down to the British and Americans still struggling in the Lower Works. As the British defenders split into smaller groups, some surrendered immediately, while others continued to resist as they sought their companions or a way to escape. Major Hull wrote later that 'we were compelled to continue the dreadful slaughter, owing to the fierce and obstinate resistance of the enemy'.[12]

As the firing ended and shouting subsided men from Butler's column filtered into the Upper Works while others, assisted by Murfree's North Carolina companies cleared the Lower Works, bringing groups of prisoners into the Upper Works. While the Americans were securing the Upper Works and eliminating up isolated pockets of resistance Captain Henry Fishbourne

10 Quoted in Dawson, *Assault on Stony Point*, p.241.
11 Quoted in Dawson, *Assault on Stony Point*, p.242.
12 Quoted in Campbell, *Revolutionary Services and Civil Life of General William Hull*, p.163.

and Henry Archer, a civilian aide to Wayne, carried the wounded brigadier general into the Upper Works. Mounting the parapet, bloodied and unsteady, Wayne received 'three long and loud cheers … reverberating in the stillness of the night'.[13] Watching the drama being played out on Stony Point were the crew of the *Vulture* and the garrison of Verplank's Point. Hearing the cheers they responded with their own in response, thinking the British garrison had repulsed the attack. They were quickly disabused of their assumption when the Continental artillerymen who had accompanied the assault columns turned the British artillery against the boats and Verplank's Point. In order to fire the guns the Americans needed access to the British gunpowder. The British artillery officer with the key to the powder magazine at first refused to cooperate, claiming he only took orders from Lieutenant Colonel Johnson. After being reminded that Johnson was no longer in command he was told the key should be produced 'or the consequences might be unpleasant'. Shortly afterwards the artillery on Stony Point began firing in earnest across the Hudson River. The dismayed crews of the British ships in the Hudson River slipped from their cables and silently rode the current out of range.

From the recollections and testimony of both Americans and British it is apparent that Febiger's attack column outpaced Butler's command in the rush towards the Upper Works. Having avoided the Lower Works abatis, Febiger's men moved quickly up the hillside towards the Upper Works abatis. Although more than double the size of Butler's group, Febiger's men appear to have maintained their compact formation and focus on the Upper Works. The company of the 17th Foot assigned to defend the abatis to the right of the Upper Works, the area that Butler's men would have advanced through, reported no movement to their front at the same time as they were aware of a growing firefight to their left as Febiger's men scrambled up the hillside and the advance elements began to carve an opening in the abatis. The commander of the British company took it on his own initiative to redeploy his men to the left, away from the path of Butler's advance, to meet this growing threat. Given Butler's order to Gibbon to move towards the center of the Upper Works the British company commander may well have seen Americans crossing his front to the left.

Butler's column was likely delayed for several reasons. Unlike Febiger's men Butler found it necessary to break through the abatis protecting the right flank of both the Upper and Lower Works. The resistance along the Lower Works abatis on the British right was much more organized and stubborn than on the left. While Febiger's column was subject to scattered fire from the picquets as they retired Butler's men faced a more determined resistance. As Gibbon's forlorn hope approached the abatis they were opposed by elements of the 71st Highlanders, who appear to have recovered after their initial surprise and engaged in protracted musket fire against the Americans struggling through the abatis. In addition to fire from the Highlanders, the 3lb gun deployed between the Upper and Lower Works, focused most of its fire at Butler's men. It is likely that rather than pushing through as a single column, a portion of Butler's men drifted towards the center and penetrated

---

13   Quoted in Campbell, *Revolutionary Services and Civil Life of General William Hull*, p.163.

the abatis near Fleche #3, while the remainder pushed through the abatis further north, across the ground above the shoreline.

Various British survivors reported encountering American troops in the Lower Works, near Fleches #2 and #3. Having their path back to the Upper Works blocked by American troops Corporal John Ash's 12-man picket spent the night hiding near the ferry landing and surrendered some time after dawn. As they were being led towards the Upper Works a Continental officer pointed to an area between Fleche #2 and the 3lb cannon, near the center of the Lower Works and lamented 'many a good Man had fallen on that Spot the Night before'.[14] Although the fracturing of Butler's column slowed its progress towards the Upper Works, the American light infantry that remained in the Lower Works had the unintended consequence of disrupting the ability of the British troops in the Lower Works to rally, reorganize and move up in support of the men in the Upper Works as Lieutenant Colonel Johnson had ordered. Each time British officers in the Lower Works tried to collect enough men to return to the Upper Works they ran into groups of wandering American light infantry, who promptly dispersed or captured the defenders.

Several days after the battle, Colonel Febiger wrote a lengthy description of the action challenging the claim of Lieutenant Gibbons, who led the forlorn hope of Butler's column, that his group of 20 men had suffered 17 casualties during their attack on the abatis. In his description Febiger also claimed that Gibbons men 'instead of advancing with musquettes unloaded, halted outside of the enemy's main Works and kept up a fire'.[15] Febiger's claim does not appear in the recollections of any other officer present that night and if true would have constituted a serious violation of the explicit order not to engage in musketry. Lieutenant Gibbon, in his account of the attack, claimed that after penetrating the abatis of the Lower Works and beginning to make his way towards the Upper Works, Lieutenant Colonel Steward 'came up and ordered me to wheel to the right and advance by sections till we came to an abbattis, cher D fries [sic – chevaux-de-frise] and Battery on which were 8 or 9 guns'.[16] Steward's directive put Gibbon's men on a path that would have encountered British troops trying to make their way to the Upper Works. Gibbon related that over the next 20 minutes he took 40 prisoners, but reaffirmed that 'we went with unloaded arms and were to depend on the bayonet'.[17]

In his account of the attack, Febiger addressed the issue of timing, writing 'that both columns did not meet in the center of the enemy's works at the same instant', that he met 'Capt. Jordan, of Stewart's battalion, just entering the works 2, which was at least 8 or 10 minutes after Colo. Johnson had surrendered' and that 'the right column led by Posey had full possession of the Fort previous to even a single man of the left being in'.[18]

---

14   Quoted in Loprieno, *The Enterprise in Contemplation*, p.234.
15   Quoted in Johnson, *Storming of Stony Point*, p.183.
16   Quoted in Dawson, *Assault on Stony Point*, p.197
17   Quoted in Dawson, *Assault on Stony Point*, p.197
18   Quoted in Johnson, *Storming of Stony Point*, p.184.

Most British witnesses estimated that from the first exchange of musket fire to the point at which the Upper Works were occupied by the Americans, 20-25 minutes elapsed. American officers estimated from the time between the first shot to last shot at 30-35 minutes. At 2.00 am 16 July Wayne sat down to write a note to Washington. Wayne was succinct, writing, 'The fort and Garrison with Col. Johnson are ours. Our men & Officers behaved like men who are determined to be free'.[19]

---

19   Quoted in Dawson, *Assault on Stony Point*, p.74

9

Aftermath

With dawn came a depressing scene of devastation and death. Detachments of American light infantry continued to round up British stragglers and add them to those already in captivity. Other detachments began collected the wounded who were cared for by a combination of Continental and British surgeons. The dead, both American and British, lay where they had fallen, waiting for yet another detail to remove them for burial. Wayne's Light Infantry Corps suffered 13 dead and 64 wounded. The bulk of the losses came from Febiger's column, accounting for 53 dead and wounded.

British losses were more severe, with 63 dead and another 61 wounded. 543 prisoners were taken, including six identified as American deserters. They were separated for later court martial Wayne's men captured two standards from the 17th Foot and two other flags, probably belonging to the Loyalist troops attached to the garrison. Despite the greater number of dead, the British were surprised that more men had not been killed. Given the severity of fight for fixed positions, garrisons resisting an enemy attack were typically at high risk of being killed. The attackers, inflamed by the adrenaline that accompanies the fear and terror of combat, particularly hand to hand fighting, found it difficult to stop the carnage, even when the enemy surrendered. The British subsequently gave a great deal of credit to the American troops for not inflicting more casualties on their defenseless captives.

In the early morning of 16 July Lieutenant Colonel Johnson was held in his tent, attended to by several American officers. Major Hull was a frequent visitor to the tent and overheard Johnson respond to a comment that the garrison had been surprised. Johnson noted 'that the firing commenced before we passed marsh, that all his men were at their stations, with their arms, and completely dressed, before our columns began to ascend the hill'. Johnson claimed 'his works were too extensive; that the they were planned for a much larger number of troops than Sir Henry Clinton had left for their defence, and that he was perfectly satisfied that his men had done their duty' [1]

At daylight Wayne's aide Captain Henry Fishboune mounted a borrowed horse and rode to Washington's headquarters at New Windsor to deliver the short note Wayne had scribbled earlier that morning. An exuberant

---

1   Quoted in Johnson, *Storming of Stony Point*, p. 193.

Washington immediately fired off a volley of letters to his immediate subordinates passing along Wayne's good news. He also sent Wayne's short note to the President of Congress, John Jay, with a promise to provide more details as they became known. A glowing Order of the Day was issued to the entire Army, in which Washington requested 'the Brigadier and his whole corps to accept his warmest thanks for the good conduct and signal bravery manifested upon the occasion'.[2] He then placed Major General William Heath in temporary command of the Continental forces around West Point and headed for Stony Point.

While Washington was making his way to Stony Point, Wayne was preparing another, slightly longer, letter, providing more detail on the events of the previous evening. Wayne passed along a return of the British killed, wounded, and prisoners, as well as the ordinance and stores captured. In this note Wayne touched briefly on a subject that would become contentious over the next several months. In his summary Wayne identified several officers for their 'bravery and fortitude'. He mentioned Febiger and Butler, was well as Fleury, Steward, and Meigs, while noting that Lieutenant Colonel Hay was wounded. Wayne apologized for lack of detail, mentioning that 'the pain I feel from a Wound in my Head prevents me from being more particular'.[3]

Washington, accompanied by Major Generals Greene and Von Steuben, arrived at Stony Point late on 17 July. By that time Wayne had prepared a more detailed description of the battle for Washington's review. While Wayne latest report provided a more detailed description of the march from Sandy Beach to their jump off positions adjacent to Stony Point he provided no specific information concerning the actual assault. In the letter Wayne reaffirmed his praise for Butler, Meigs, Steward, Fleury, and Febiger, adding recognition of the leaders of the forlorn hopes, Gibbons and Knox. Wayne also mentioned his aides, Fishbourne and Archer, and thanked Major Lee for his assistance in collecting information about the Stony Point defenses. This 17 July letter, coupled with the shorter note sent late on 16 July, would form the basis for Washington's message to Congress. It would also be used by the various newspapers throughout the colonies to report on the Continental victory. Wayne's omission, intentional or not, of other officers and lack of specific details about the attack would be the subject of contentious debate in the near future. By not publicly recognizing some of the officers so that their contributions were included in Washington's report to Congress, the standing of those officers before Congress was diminished, as was opportunity for future promotion. Similarly, by not being included in the public newspapers accounts of the attack, these officers might believe their honor was besmirched.

While at Stony Point Washington made a point of exploring the entire battlefield and meeting with the officers. Major Hull remembered 'how cordially he took us by the hand, and the satisfaction and the joy that glowed in his countenance'. Washington was particularly interested in the paths taken by both assault columns, the difficulty of the ascent, and the minimal loss of life in the effort. Washington 'offered his thanks to Almighty God, that

2   'General Orders, 16 July 1779,' *Founders Online*, National Archives.
3   Wayne to Washington, 16 July 1779,' *Founders Online*, National Archives.

he had been our shield and protector, amidst the danger we had been called to encounter'.[4] Wayne, still suffering from his head wound, was unable to join Washington and his fellow officers.

At New Windsor on 16 July, after receiving news of Wayne's capture of Stony Point Washington put the second phase of his plan to secure Kings Ferry into motion. He wrote Major General Robert Howe, directing him to begin operations against Verplank's Point, the object being to capture the strong point or force the British to abandon the fort.

Washington had originally hoped to attack both Stony Point and Verplank's Point simultaneously, but he realized the complexity of coordinating both attacks was beyond the capabilities of his staff. Rather than a full scale attack Washington had ordered Colonel Rufus Putnam with a detachment of Nixon's brigade to undertake a diversionary attack on Verplank's Point on the night of 15 July, in conjunction with Wayne's attack. After observing Wayne's attack Putnam fired on the British sentries and blockhouse at Verplank's Point, creating enough noise to cause the garrison alarm, before retiring the next morning back to Continental Village.

With the attack on Stony Point resulting in a crowning success Washington looked forward to repeating his success at Verplank's Point. He instructed Major General Howe to take command of Brigadier Generals Nixon and Patterson at Continental Village, and then move his command to Peekskill.

Robert Howe, 47, was the highest ranking Continental officer from North Carolina. Although serving in the North Carolina militia, Howe made his living as a planter, and was a member of both the North Carolina legislature and a delegate to the 1774 Colonial Congress. Commissioned a colonel in 1775 he and Colonel Woodford of Virginia commanded the Continental force that captured Norfolk, Virginia. For that success he was promoted to brigadier general by Congress in 1777. He commanded at Charleston and then was promoted to major general and placed in charge of the Southern Department in October 1777. After a disappointing expedition to Florida, in which he engaged in ongoing disputes with the Governor of Georgia and militia officers over control of the Georgia militia, Howe's disease-ridden command retreated to Charleston. Howe's very public disputes with elected officials, including a a duel with South Carolina Lieutenant Governor Christopher Gadsden, and private indiscretions led to his being replaced by Major General Benjamin Lincoln in September, 1778. Howe assumed command at Savanah, where he was attacked in December, 1778, the city falling to British assault on 29 December. Howe was widely criticized for the loss and although a court-martial exonerated him, Howe returned to the Northern Department, where he was assigned to West Point.

At Peekskill Washington directed Howe to begin to develop a plan for assaulting Verplank's Point. Washington recommended that Howe conduct a thorough reconnaissance and identify the best approaches to attack the position and where best to deploy his artillery to support his attack. Rather than undertake these activities surreptitiously, Washington proposed that Howe do so in full view of the British, hoping that the prospect of an

4   Quoted in Campbell, *Revolutionary Services and Civil Life of General William Hull*, pp.166-7.

American assault would be enough to induce them to abandon the position. Washington requested Howe provide him with updates on his activities and warned him to keep watch on British movements either up the Hudson River or a possible attack Connecticut against his left flank. He added a postscript ordering Howe to 'take with you the field pieces belonging to the Brigades – & two 12 pounders ordered to Nelsons point'.[5]

The attempt to take Verplank's Point misfired from the beginning, lacking any semblance of the meticulous planning and attention to detail that characterized Washington and Wayne's effort to attack Stony Point. After his successful diversion at Verplank's Point Colonel Putnam returned to Continental Village later on 16 July and found Nixon's and Patterson's brigades, 'without there feld peaces, artillerymen or so much as an ax or Spade, or any ordors what they were to do'. Howe arrived at Continental Village at 10.00 pm. and summoned Putnam, who told him if he was going to attack Verplank's Point he would need artillery and tools to rebuild a bridge over the Croton River, neither of which Nixon or Patterson had brought with them.

On 17 July Howe and Washington exchanged a series of letters as Washington tried to make Howe understand the subtle nuances of the directive to capture Verplank's Point. Washington understood that time was working against the American efforts and Clinton should be expected to react quickly and dramatically to the humiliating loss of Stony Point. Howe began the exchange early on 17 July, informing Washington he had arrived at Continental Village and learned Brigadier General Nixon claimed to have never been assigned artillery whilst Patterson had belatedly ordered his guns to join his brigade at Continental Village. He asked Washington to expedite the arrival of the promised 12lb guns and pointed out that Colonel Putnam warned him that taking a position at Peekskill might put his command at risk of being cut off since they had no cavalry to act as pickets to watch British movements.

Washington responded by outlining for Howe the steps of a plan to invest the fort, directing him to use his artillery to destroy the blockhouse, surround the British position, and give the appearance he was ready to storm the fort. Howe should demand the fort surrender but not attempt an assault during daylight. At the same time Washington issued a cautionary note, warning Howe to be alert to a possible British offensive and recommended he post sentries along two possible routes the British might use to advance around his left flank. If threatened, Howe was directed to retreat to Continental Village. Washington also told Howe to apply to Major General William Heath for a detachment of cavalry.

To his credit Howe made his way south to look at Verplank's Point and provided Washington with another, longer list enumerating the difficulties he faced. He hoped the 12lb cannon would arrive later that day, but he had been informed Patterson's guns would not arrive by the end of the day and reminded Washington he would also need appropriate ammunition for the guns. He pointed out that if he needed to prepare works he would need entrenching tools and complained his men had no provisions, asking

---

5   Washington to Howe, 16 July 1779, *Founders Online,* National Archives.

Washington to send wagons with the necessary supplies. He told Washington he had requested cavalry from Major General Heath but in their absence was utilizing local militia to safeguard the routes. Finally, his engineers had examined Verplank's Point and confirmed Washington's assessment that an outright assault was out of the question.

Late in the day, with both notes from Howe in his possession Washington wrote to express his concern for Howe's difficulties. He assured him the cannon, which did arrive late on 17 July, should be making their way to him, along with ammunition, pointing out the obvious, 'as One without the other would be of no service'. He promised to send the entrenching tools and some provisions from West Point and he confirmed Howe should not expect a detachment of cavalry from Heath and should endeavor to utilize the militia cavalry as necessary. Finally he passed along intelligence that the British forces around New York were on the move, advancing north towards White Plains, and cautioned Howe to rely on Colonel Putnam and 'rely much in his Judgement'.[6]

Washington's frustration over the management of the Continental artillery, both in supporting Howe's attack on Verplank's Point and in removing the heavy cannon captured at Stony Point, came to a head after he requested on 16 July the Commanding Office of Artillery at Chester, New York provide horses and harnesses. Major General Alexander McDougall responded the next day notifying Washington that there were no horse harnesses to be had at New Windsor or Newburgh and that the harnesses used to pull wagons would not work for artillery.

The issue of the artillery became moot late on 18 July when Howe penned a quick note to Washington passing along information that the British were marching north in force and that their objective was to trap him. Unwilling to make the decision to abandon his position unilaterally Howe held a council of war with his brigadier generals, who, not surprisingly, advised immediate retreat. With that Howe ordered a retirement. On 19 July Washington wrote, in no little frustration, to Major General Heath, who had arrived at Peekskill just in time to join Howe as he began his retreat, directing him to return the two 12lb guns back to New Windsor. The attempt to capture Verplank's Point was over.

Howe never appeared to understand the complexity or sense of urgency connected with Washington's plan. For Washington's part, unlike the close coordination with Wayne there is no record that Washington had conversations with Howe about the attack prior to ordering him to take command of the attack force at Continental Village. Washington gave some insight into the delay in initiating the attack in his later message to Congress. Washington ordered that all messages to him from Wayne should be routed through Major General McDougall, who was to read the letters before sending along to Washington. In this way McDougall would have received notice of Wayne's success early on the morning of 16 July and been able to initiate the attack on Verplank's Point immediately. Unfortunately Wayne's courier, Captain Fishbourne, did not ride to McDougall but directly to

---

6   Washington to Howe, 17 July 1779, *Founders Online,* National Archives.

headquarters at New Windsor, leaving Washington to belatedly pass along the news to McDougall.

Although valuable time had been lost, the euphoria of the victory at Stony Point emboldened Washington to initiate the effort against Verplank's Point. The subsequent delays in allocating the necessary artillery and entrenching tools are inexplicable if McDougall had been briefed and was standing by to hear from Wayne. The choice of Howe as overall commander of the attack is also puzzling since there is no record that Washington discussed the attack with him. Washington tried to pass along his thinking in his correspondence with Howe, but with minimal preparation undertaken for the attack Washington needed a commander who could respond quickly and who understood the fundamental elements that were required. Howe was not that commander. Brigadier General William Irvine commented that Howe had 'a talent … of finding many supposed obstructions and barely plausible pretences for his delay'.[7]

Along with an examination of the British defenses Washington and his aides were also interested in a cataloging of the stores and equipment taken by Wayne's men. In addition to capturing the British fortifications, American troops spent 16 July collecting the stores and equipment. A total of 15 cannon were taken, along with 334 muskets, 30,000 musket cartridges ,and various artillery rounds. 140 tents, various entrenching tools and all manner of cooking camp equipment were also collected. Six musical instruments, valued at over $1,000, were captured. The estimated value of the ordinance and stores was $158,640. Proceeds from an additional $22,015 in captured material were distributed proportionately to every member of the force. The payments ranged from $78.92 for each private to $1,420.51 going to Wayne, both amounts representing nearly a year's salary. Some officers, such as Major Hull, secured additional rewards. In Hull's case he reported acquiring a complete camp equipage, which included a marquee tent, bed and mattress, a large pair of horse canteens, various plates, and other furniture.

Anticipating the challenges in finding transport for the materials, on 16 July Colonel Alexander Hamilton, Washington's aide, had directed Captain Allen McLane to collect horses and wagons in the adjacent area to remove the cannon, stores, and wounded. Despite these preparations the American determined they needed to employ ships to carry the heaviest cannon upriver to West Point. All but one of the heavy cannon were successfully moved to West Point in the next several days. The last gun, kept at Stony Point in case of a British attack, was loaded on the row galley *Lady Washington*. The galley, weighed down with its cargo and struggling against a contrary wind, became an easy target for the British cannon at Verplank's Point, causing it to run aground. Throwing the cannon overboard to lighten the load failed to free the *Lady Washington*, which was abandoned and burned.

Controversy over imagined and real slights in the reporting of the battle and the distribution of receipts from the captured stores began almost immediately. On 30 July Major Henry Lee wrote Wayne complaining, 'My feelings are very much hurt by a report which Capt. Handy has communicated

---

7   Quoted in Hugh Rankin, *The North Carolina Continentals* (Chapel Hill: University of North Carolina Press, 1971), p.74.

to me, viz. that the three companys of Infantry under my command which join'd you on the night of the 15th are to be excluded from a share of the booty'.[8]

At about the same time on 24 July Washington responded to Colonel Nathaniel Gist of the Virginia line, who wrote to Washington raising the issue of rumors that members of the Virginia line, which supported Wayne's attack and entered the Stony Point grounds to assist in securing the prisoners and material, had taken some of the captured stores. Washington replied by claiming that while he had heard the same insinuations he had no firm evidence and no intention of pursuing the matter. He did tell Gist that if he felt an inquiry was necessary Washington would 'cheerfully' order an investigation. The more pressing issue raised by Gist was whether his men were entitled to any of the prize money. While Washington admitted that each situation should be evaluated on its own merits the circumstances of Wayne's attack were clear and Gist's men acted as a 'covering party in Case of Accident and to give countenance to the Assailants rather than as a body of support'.[9]

More troubling was a lengthy complaint prepared by Major Posey and submitted to Washington in early August. Posey wrote that, after reviewing Washington's announcement to Congress, which was based on the descriptions prepared by Wayne, he felt 'a most Sensiable Mortification; and am most feelingly hurt, but finding my self totally Neglected'.[10]

Colonel Meigs took Wayne to task on 22 August, for not including mention of Major Hull and his participation in the assault or that other officers in addition to Lieutenant Colonel Hay had been wounded. On the same day Lieutenant Colonel Sherman took up the cause of the New England companies, accusing Wayne of partially to certain States and warning him about the 'sentiments and uneasiness of many officers under your command, which, perhaps, is more extensive than you may imagin'.[11]

Wayne responded to Meigs the next day arguing that if he was to name every officer worthy of mention he would have to include every officer of the Corps. Similarly, continuing the logic, if he should be expected to included worthy non-commissioned officers and privates 'the Absurdity is too Obvious to admit of serious comment'.[12] As a postscript Wayne included a pointed reference to the letter from Sherman, which he described being 'of a very extraordinary Nature' that would require a 'very Serious and particular explanation', adding 'I put up with no mans Insults'.[13] Meigs apparently showed Sherman Wayne's postscript, resulting in Sherman writing to claim he meant Wayne no insult but only intended to inform him that officers under his command 'imagined themselves sensibly injured'.[14]

---

8   Quoted in Dawson, *Assault on Stony Point*, p.122.
9   Washington to Gist and Officers of the Virginia Line, 24 July 1779, *Founders Online*, National Archives.
10 Quoted in Dawson, *Assault on Stony Point*, p.128.
11 Quoted in Dawson, *Assault on Stony Point*, p.133.
12 Quoted in Dawson, *Assault on Stony Point*, p.134.
13 Quoted in Dawson, *Assault on Stony Point*, p.136.
14 Quoted in Dawson, *Assault on Stony Point*, p.136.

In response to these complaints Wayne prepared a fuller description of the events of 15 July for Congress, mentioning by name Sherman, Hull and Posey. Washington passed along the letter to Congress through John Jay, which apparently put the matter to rest to the satisfaction of the aggrieved officers.

In addition to the individual awards, Wayne had promised the first five men into the Upper Works a promotion and cash reward. It was agreed that Lieutenant Colonel Fluery was the first, followed by Lieutenant Knox and then three sergeants, Baker, Spencer, and Dunlop, each of whom sustained at least two wounds. The first four of these men were from Febiger's column, while Dunlop was a member of Butler's command. In order to have entered the works at approximately the same time as others Dunlop must have separated from the larger group and scaled the parapets directly from the Lower Works rather than penetrating the Upper Works abatis and then making his way into the Upper Works through the rear section.

In addition to the material, Washington's aides, Colonels Alexander Hamilton and Tench Tilghman made arrangements for securing the prisoners. Major Lee's Legion escorted the enlisted men south to Hardytown, Pennsylvania. An ill-advised escape attempt by members of the 17th Foot resulted in nine more wounded British prisoners. Lieutenant Colonel Johnson and the British officers were similarly sent into captivity at Lancaster, Pennsylvania. Johnson and the others were considered on parole and billeted in private residences, on a promise not to escape.

While the prisoners were being marched south Wayne convened a court-marshal for the American deserters found enlisted among the British garrison. Five men were found guilty and on 18 July they were hanged at the flagpole in the Upper Works. A sixth captive was not tried and may have been an American spy, sent to infiltrate the garrison in order to gather information.

On that same day the American light infantry completed dismantling and burning the British fortifications at Stony Point. Despite his delight at having captured Stony Point, and understanding that West Point would be at risk as long as the British occupied the hilltop fort, Washington knew he could not keep it. The subsequent failure of the effort to capture Verplank's Point ended any illusion might have had about defending Stony Point. Possession of Verplank's Point gave the British a foothold at Kings Ferry, from which they could deny the movement of supplies and material across the Hudson River, while also providing Clinton a jumping-off point for future operations. As Washington later explained to Congress, garrisoning Stony Point would have required approximately 1,500 men, men the army could ill afford to lose. In addition the fortifications would require extensive improvements, particularly to guard against an assault from the Hudson River. More importantly Washington was still anxious about the safety of West Point and issued orders on 19 July for a redeployment of the Continental Army.

Clinton, for his part, was indeed in motion. When the news reached him at mid-morning, 16 July, his 'astonishment could not be but extreme' since he assumed, given the natural strength of Stony Point, defending the position 'required little more than vigilance in its garrison' and he 'looked on the place as perfectly secure with the works already there, especially as it was under the charge of a vigilant, active and spirited office and a very ample garrison'.[15] The loss of Stony Point was accompanied by news that Verplank's Point was being threatened.

Shaking off his initial shock, on 17 July Clinton ordered the army to advance to Dobbs Ferry and dispatched a mixed force of cavalry, light infantry and grenadiers to advance further to the Croton River and relieve Verplank's Point. Another detachment under Brigadier General Stirling was assigned to advance towards Stony Point to either rescue the garrison or recapture the position. Clinton later added Hessian and Loyalist units, as well as artillery, to Stirling's column and joined the flotilla, which struggled under a north wind to sail to Stony Point. Clinton held out some hope that the loss of Stony Point might eventually yield unintended benefits if he could induce Washington to give battle. He was therefore disappointed when he sailed into Haverstraw Bay on 20 July to find the Washington and his forces had abandoned Stony Point. Colonel Butler, now temporarily in command of the Light Corps while Wayne continued to recover from his wound, reported the British reoccupation to Washington.

Clinton assigned the 42nd Highlanders and 63rd and 64th Foot, nearly 1,500 men, to garrison Stony Point, while adding an additional 700 men, including four companies from Colonel Edmund Fanning's Loyalist Kings American Regiment to the existing garrison of Verplank's Point. Captain Mercer, the engineer who had designed the original Stony Point defenses accompanied the relief column and on meeting Lieutenant Colonel Webster, commander of the Verplank's Point garrison exclaimed, 'Good God! Colonel Webster, did I not always say that these Points ought not be defended?'[16]

Once the crisis had passed Clinton was able to admit his mortification at the unfolding events at Stony Point. 'The success attending this bold and well-combined attempt of the enemy procured very deservedly no small share of reputation and applause to the spirited officer (General Wayne) who conducted it'.[17]

Adding to Clinton's distress in the aftermath of the debacle at Stony Point, Lieutenant General Cornwallis arrived on 21 July with dispatches from Germain. Written in early May, St. German passed along information concerning the sailing of a French taskforce carrying an estimated 3,000 troops. While their destination was unknown Germain suspected they might be bound for Canada. Germain also confirmed what Clinton already knew, that his promised reinforcements from England had been delayed. Germain explained the problem was a combination of contrary winds and the need for Arbuthnot's fleet to respond to a French attack on Jersey Island. The setback at Stony Point, coupled with the reduction in overall reinforcements and expected delay in the arrival of the remaining reinforcements, combined to remove any further illusion from Clinton's mind that he could strike any meaningful blow against Washington in the short time remaining in the campaigning year.

---

15 Clinton, *The American Rebellion*, pp.131-132.
16 Quoted in Loprieno, *The Enterprise in Contemplation*, p.252.
17 Quoted in Loprieno, *The Enterprise in Contemplation*, p.133.

Washington was still wary of Clinton's intentions. Butler was of the opinion that the British were preparing to push north to West Point. Washington alerted McDougall to that possibility, particularly if 'Sir Harry [Clinton] may wish to retaliate for the loss of that post. I am therefore extremely anxious that we should be prepared to receive them'.[18] Washington ordered Butler to continue to monitor activities at Stony Point, gathering information about the extent of the new defenses and size of the garrison. He issued a similar request to Major General Heath to collect intelligence on the status of the Verplank's Point garrison.

On 26 July Washington held a meeting of his senior officers: after providing information on the current state of the Continental Army, and intelligence on British dispositions, he outlined several possible courses of action the British might take. Washington believed Clinton might still be interested in attacking West Point and in the process engage the Continental Army or conversely, his primary objective might be forcing the Army to fight. If the Continental Army was the objective, the British might attempt to dislodge it from its strong defensive positions around West Point by either threatening the American lines of communication to the west and the supply depot at Easton; or, by operating further east, in Connecticut, draw the Army away from the Hudson Valley. Washington then asked his officers whether the army should take offensive action. Implicit in Washington's request was the possibility of another attack on the Kings Ferry defenses.

As Washington had probably anticipated, the senior officers duly replied with a wide variety of suggested actions the army should take but were unanimous in their opposition to any substantial offensive against the British. Major General Nathanael Greene, upon whose opinion Washington usually put great weight, did not mince words, admitting that 'we have neither force or ammunition to commence any serious operations against New York or its dependencies', and concluding that any attempt to attack the British at New York, given their secure positions and naval superiority 'will be madness in the extreme'. He reminded Washington of the critical importance of the Hudson Highlands and the need to protect both Connecticut and New Jersey. He recommended Washington detach several brigades to Connecticut to protect against further raids by the British and several to New Jersey to secure the supply base at Trenton. He proposed the Light Infantry Corps monitor British activity around the Kings Ferry and the remainder of the army concentrate on completing the fortifications at West Point. Beyond that, Greene felt that any action against Verplank's Point would 'rather serve to amuse the public, than procure any solid advantage'.[19]

Washington dutifully took Greene's advice and issued orders on 29 July to redeploy a portion of the Army to defend Connecticut and New Jersey, as well as directing the Army redouble its efforts to complete the West Point works. Unable to completely dismiss the intriguing possibility that the success at Stony Point might be repeated, Washington continued to flirt with the idea of another effort against the fort. He wrote to Wayne on 30 July, apparently in response to a note from Wayne requesting Washington not initiate any

---

18   George Washington to McDougall, 20 July 1779, *Founders Online,* National Archives.
19   Greene to Washington, 27 July 1779, *Founders Online,* National Archives.

major actions without him. After assuring Wayne that 'I shall certainly not undertake any thing (capital) without your knowledge' Washington asked directly for Wayne's opinion as to 'whether another attempt upon Stoney point by way of surprise, is eligible'.[20] Always eager to take the offense, Wayne replied with a decidedly minority opinion on 31 July. Wayne admitted the British had learned their lessons from the previous attack and undoubtedly had strengthened the most vulnerable parts of the Stony Point defenses, including fully enclosing the Upper Works. But even at that 'I am of Opinion that the Light Corps with the Addition of One Thousand more picked men and officers properly Appointed would cary that post by Assault in the night with the loss of between four and five Hundred men'. He added, despite his wound, he would 'cheerfully undertake the charge'.[21] Colonel Butler, meeting Washington at Sandy Beach the next day reported to Wayne, that Washington 'has a Wish to try the new family of Stony Point' which Butler agreed was practicable but also thought would result in significant casualties.[22]

Washington continued to monitor British activity at Kings Ferry. At Washington's behest Wayne reported regularly through August and September on British progress to improve the defenses. In late September it appeared from British movements they might be about to abandon Verplank's Point but Washington ultimately concluded on 20 September that although the British had transferred units away from the forts the result was only a contraction of their lines.

Wayne, ever concerned about the appearance of his men, proposed on 14 September that the Light Corps be uniformed in blue coats with red facings, complaining that many of his men's uniforms were ragged and some reduced to wearing linen hunting shirts. Washington's response reflected his continued reluctance to create a permanent organization for the light infantry, something Wayne had encouraged on several occasions. Washington wrote 'The Light Infantry being only considered as detachments from the line ought to bear the uniform of the Regiments from which they are taken'.[23]

Nevertheless Washington ordered Wayne to conduct a thorough reconnaissance of Stony Point on 26 September and sent along Major General Henry Knox, commander of the artillery, and Brigadier General Louis Duportail, chief engineer. Knox reported back to Washington on 30 September, providing his assessment. He recommended at least 16 heavy cannon and ten mortars would be required to overwhelm the defenses on Stony Point. He included an estimate of the required ammunition and reminded Washington that the forces besieging Stony Point should be large enough to protect the artillery from a British relief force. He was more optimistic about Verplank's Point, noting the British had contracted their defenses, and he concluded American artillery could force the garrison to either surrender or abandon the works.

---

20 Washington to Wayne, 30 July 1779, *Founders Online,* National Archives.
21 Wayne to Washington, 31 July 1779, *Founders Online,* National Archives.
22 Quoted in editorial footnote to Wayne to Washington, 31 July 1779, *Founders Online,* National Archives.
23 Washington to Wayne, 14 September 1779, *Founders Online,* National Archives.

By this time Washington had turned his attention back to Stony Point, contemplating a siege as part of a possible joint operation in conjunction with the expected arrival of a French fleet. Washington's ongoing interest in the defenses of the Kings Ferry forts reflected a much broader strategy. In mid-July, prior to the Stony Point attack, with news that French forces under Vice Admiral d'Estaing were preparing to sail to America, Washington wrote d'Estaing, eliciting his support for a joint attack on the British in New York. After receiving erroneous intelligence in early September that d'Estaing's fleet had arrived off the American coast, Washington issued orders for a portion of the army to move into position to hinder any British withdrawal from the Kings Ferry defenses. At the same time Washington wrote to d'Estaing, recommending sailing into New York harbor and landing troops on either Staten Island or Long Island. After securing New York harbor Washington requested d'Estaing sail several frigates up the Hudson to Haverstraw Bay to support his efforts to block the retreat of British troops south to Kings Bridge.

By 18 September Washington confirmed news of d'Estaing's arrival was premature and he cancelled the movements of Major Generals Heath and Howe. By early October Washington had crafted a detailed plan for coordinating an attack on the British defenses around New York in conjunction with d'Estaing's task force. Wayne provided Washington with a constant stream of information on the Stony Point defenses and passed along information on 14 October that Clinton had sailed up from New York to inspect the works. A week later, on 21 October, Washington alerted Wayne to the surprising news that the British had abandoned both Stony Point and Verplank's Point. The next day Wayne and the Light Corps reoccupied Stony Point.

The impact of Stony Point reverberated throughout the American Colonies and in England. As much as this was a victory of arms it was also a propaganda success. American newspapers carried glowing stories of the success of Washington and the Continental Army. Although Loyalist newspapers tried to play down the consequences of the defeat, it was difficult to minimize the shock and dismay experienced by Clinton and his Loyalist allies.

On 21 July Washington submitted his official report on the capture of Stony Point to the Continental Congress. To begin the report Washington heaped praise on Wayne, writing 'his own conduct, throughout the whole of this arduous enterprise, merits the warmest approbation of Congress. He improved upon the plan recommended by me and executed it in a manner, that does signal honor to his judgement and to his bravery'. Washington explained his motivation for ordering the attack, primarily to deny Clinton the use of Kings Ferry, but also recognizing 'the necessity of doing something to satisfy the expectations of the people and reconcile them to the defensive plan we are obliged to pursue, and to the inactivity, which our situation imposes upon us'. Claiming he had every expectation of success he suggested the 'probably disadvantages of a failure were comparatively inconsiderable' and might amount to a small loss of men.

A large section of the report reviewed the reasons the attack against Verplank's Point failed and why reoccupying Stony Point was, on balance, not justified. After enumerating the material and ordinance taken at Stony Point Washington admitted the British had reoccupied Stony Point shortly after he abandoned it, but insisted that constructing new fortifications and properly garrisoning the fort would require substantial time and resources that would limit Clinton's ability to engage in other actions such as repeating the devastating raids into Virginia and Connecticut. He reminded Congress that the protection of West Point remained his highest priority and had positioned the army to protect against any attack by the British. To illustrate his concern for West Point, Washington announced he would be moving his headquarters there immediately.

He concluded the report by singling out Lieutenant Colonel Fleury and Major Steward, who commanded the advance guards, and the leaders of the forlorn hopes, Captains Gibbons and Knox. He also recognized Wayne's volunteer aide, Henry Archer, who was given the honor to deliver the report to Congress, describing him as a 'Gentleman of merit'. Washington had previously asked Wayne to recommend which aide, Archer or Captain Fishbourne, should deliver his report, noting Archer held no commission in the Army, which he found 'peculiar'. Wayne recommended Archer seemingly because he held no rank but the best explanation for selecting Archer may have been to protect Captain Fishbourne from embarrassment. In explaining the missteps associate with the failed attempt to capture Verplank's Point Washington's report rested on the error made by Wayne's messenger in failing to carry notice of capture of the fort to Major General McDougall rather than to him. This error led to a fatal delay in the movement of Major General Howe to invest Verplank's Point. Captain Fishbourne was the messenger who failed to deliver the message to McDougall. In any case Washington recommended Congress extend the rank of captain to Archer.[24]

On 26 July, Congress passed a resolution recognizing Wayne, his officers and men, and in keeping with the customs of the time authorized the production of special medallions, gold for Wayne and silver for Fleury and Steward. Until that time only two other medals had been awarded, one to Washington for his successful siege of Boston and another to Major General Horatio Gates for his victory at Saratoga.

The reverberations of the loss of Stony Point were not limited to America. It was not until 25 July that Clinton finally set down the events of 15 July for the British government. Beginning with a reminder of his need for reinforcements Clinton provided a cursory description of the loss of Stony Point, passing along Lieutenant Colonel Johnson's account which he had prepared while in captivity. Clinton described in greater detail the successful defense of Verplank's Point and emphasized his prompt response to the loss of Stony Point.

News about the defeat at Stony Point began to find its way back to England through other sources. British artilleryman Brigadier General James Pattison wrote on 26 July to Lord Townsend, notifying him of the action and providing information on the units involved and number of men lost. As other British officers would do, Pattison gave grudging praise to Wayne, writing 'it must in justice be allow'd to his credit, as well as to all acting under

---

24   Washington to John Jay, 21 July 1779, *Founders Online,* National Archives.

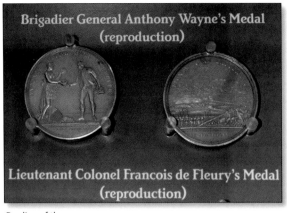

Brigadier General Anthony Wayne's Medal (reproduction)

Lieutenant Colonel Francois de Fleury's Medal (reproduction)

Replica of the commemorative medal struck by Congress for Anthony Wayne in honor of the Stony Point attack. (Author's Photo)

his Orders, that no instance of Inhumanity was shown to any of the unhappy Captives'.[25]

Commodore George Collier wrote that Tyron was forced to abandon plans to continue the attacks in Connecticut with the news of the loss of Stony Point. He was also complimentary of the Americans, claiming 'the enterprise of really a gallant one, and as bravely executed' admitting, 'the rebels had made the attack with a bravery they never before exhibited, and they showed at this moment a generosity and clemency which during the course of the rebellion had no parallel'.[26]

Clinton prepared a letter on 20 August primarily in response to the directives Cornwallis had brought with him. He began his letter expressing his happiness that Lord Cornwallis had returned from England and then took the opportunity of Cornwallis' arrival to request he be relieved of command. As he had in his previous request for relief Clinton told Germain 'my spirits are worn out by struggling against the Consequences of many adverse incidents, without appearing publicly to account for my situation, have effectually oppressed me'. He immediately returned to the issue of reinforcements affirming that the only new troops he might expect were two newly-raised regiments and whatever forces he might recruit from the Loyalist population. At the same time, he reminded Germain, 'I am obliged to send two thousand men to men to Canada'.[27]

The next day, almost as a postscript, Clinton penned another letter to Germain raising again the issue of the lack of the expected reinforcements and how that had resulted in Clinton having to abandon his plans an offensive in the Hudson Valley during the current campaign season.

Several days later, on 25 August, Arbuthnot's fleet limped into New York, carrying two newly-recruited regiments, part of another regiment and replacements for seven other regiments, totaling approximately 3,800 men. In addition to being far short of the 6,600 men Clinton believed he had been promised these men carried with them a malignant fever, which spread to the rest of the army, putting 6,000 men in the hospital.

In early September, Clinton wrote to his counterpart, Major General Haldimand, commander of the Canadian theater, to unburden himself about his efforts over the summer and review how things went awry. Clinton claimed he had stolen a march on Washington, opening his offensive several weeks before Washington expected an attack. Having secured Kings Ferry Clinton believed Washington would defend West Point and in the process possibly put his army at risk. Clinton was clear he never intended to attack West Point, but, given Washington's supply difficulties, his objective was to capture Middlebrook, cutting off Washington's communications with his supply depots at Trenton and Easton, Pennsylvania. He admitted even success

---

25   Quoted in Johnson, *Storming of Stony Point*, p.131.
26   Quoted in Johnson, *Storming of Stony Point*, p.135.
27   Quoted in Johnson, *Storming of Stony Point*, p.139.

in capturing the magazines at Easton might not have resulted in Washington consenting to give battle and he was unable to pry the Continentals away from New Windsor. Clinton regretted that the raids into Connecticut also failed to entice Washington to move and as all his plans now required the expected return of the four regiments from the West Indies their delay, coupled with the American attack on Stony Point and the troubling news about French intervention doomed his plans. Clinton closed, writing as 'weak and miserable as I am, I am obliged to comply with your requisition, and therefore, Sir, I send you three Regiments'.[28] Clinton sent 2,000 men north with his note to Haldimand.

Alarmed at a possible French invasion of Jamaica by d'Estaing's fleet in late September, Clinton reluctantly loaded 4,000 men under the command of Cornwallis on Arbuthnot's ships and sent them south. On their way south Arbuthnot received information that the French fleet had been sighted near the Bahamas, headed north. He immediately returned to New York where both he and Clinton were alarmed by the idea that d'Estaing's destination was New York. To Clinton's relief and Washington's disappointment d'Estaing sailed for Charleston. The prospect of a French attack, coupled with the reduction of the troops defending New York was the cause of Clinton's decision to withdraw the garrisons at both Stony Point and Verplank's Point, 'whose importance of course ceased the moment I game up offensive operations in the Hudson'.[29]

---

28 Quoted in Johnson, *Storming of Stony Point,* pp.143-4.
29 Clinton, *American Rebellion*, p.47.

Epilogue

As the fall leaves turned the Hudson Valley landscape a vibrant hue of red, yellow, and orange and the chill of the wind blowing south from Canada suggested winter was close at hand, the war left the Hudson Highlands.

For Clinton the war moved not only out of the Hudson Valley but out of New York altogether and into the southern colonies. 1779 ended and 1780 began with encouraging victories in the south. The capture of both Savannah and Charleston suggested British fortunes would be decided not in the northern colonies but in Virginia and the Carolinas. In the end the war was decided in the south, but on Washington's terms not Clinton's. Just as he had failed Burgoyne in 1777, Clinton's vacillations coupled with an unreliable naval partner in Vice Admiral Arbuthnot doomed Lord Cornwallis at Yorktown and the ultimately the British cause. After being replaced in 1782 by Sir Guy Carleton, Clinton returned to England and published his *Narrative of the Campaign of 1781*, in which he attempted to lay the blame for the American debacle squarely on Cornwallis' shoulders. The publication of the *Narrative* ignited a vitriolic public debate with Cornwallis. Clinton also served several terms in Parliament, was made a full general in 1793 and died in 1795.

For Washington, like Clinton, the coming year, 1780, would be frustrating, and cause no little apprehension at the prospect that, despite having fought the British Empire to a standstill over the last five years of desultory warfare, the outcome still hung in the balance. While Wayne is most closely associated with the victory at Stony Point, it was Washington who conceived of the original plan of attack and developed the outline for the assault, which was only slightly modified by Wayne. Most importantly it was Washington who was willing, in the face of skepticism and in some cases outright opposition from his senior generals, to take the calculated risk and assault the British works at Stony Point.

Washington's success at Stony Point could have been made complete with the capture of Verplank's Point and he appeared greatly disappointed in American General Robert Howe's failure to act expeditiously to carry out his directives. The failure at Verplank's Point may have been a godsend since it is doubtful that the Continental Army could have defended both Stony Point and Verplank's Point against a determined British counter attack. Having captured the forts Washington might have found himself obliged to defend both, requiring the full commitment of the Continental Army, which might have resulted in the decisive battle that Clinton so long desired. As it was,

Washington rightly concluded that without possession of Verplank's Point the occupation of Stony Point would serve no strategic purpose and would require resources the Continental Army could ill afford. For the Continental cause the capture of Stony Point was most importantly a propaganda victory, reviving the resolve of patriots to continue the struggle, and the inability to defend the fort gave Washington a convenient reason to abandon it.

For Wayne the accolades continued. Writing immediately after the war, the British military historian Charles Stedman commented that 'the conduct of the Americans upon this occasion was highly meritorious, for they would have been fully justified in putting the garrison to the sword, not one man of which was put to death but in fair combat'.[1] With the disbanding of the Light Corps in December, 1779 Wayne returned to Pennsylvania where he spent the winter before being recalled by Washington to the command the Pennsylvania line in May, 1780. Wayne and his men struggled through a year of discontent, culminating with Wayne putting down a mutiny among his soldiers in December 1780. After spending the spring of 1781 recruiting replacements for his depleted regiments, Wayne was ordered to Virginia in early 1781 to assist Marquis Lafayette, who now commanded the newly re-formed Light Corps. Wayne fought through the Yorktown campaign and continued to serve in the Continental Army after the British surrender at Yorktown, fighting skirmishes with the British and Indians in Georgia and finally negotiating with the Creek and Cherokee tribes to end the war in the south. In return for his service the State of Georgia awarded Wayne a rice plantation. He was promoted to Major General in 1783 but left the service in 1784. After returning briefly to Pennsylvania Wayne moved to Georgia and was elected to Congress from the 1st District. President George Washington recalled Wayne to active service in 1791 in response to a series defeats at the hands of Indian tribes in the Northwest Territory. Wayne took command of the newly created Legion of the United States and defeated the Indian Confederacy at the Battle of Fallen Timbers in 1794. After his victory Wayne negotiated the Treaty of Greenville which ceded the land that encompassed the future state of Ohio to the United States. Wayne died of complications from gout in 1796.

The Light Corps was again dispersed back to their parent regiments at the end of 1779 as the army went into winter quarters. In August, 1780 Washington reformed the Corps on a more permanent basis and place it under the command of Lafayette. At his own expense Lafayette provided the Corps with a standard uniform, including distinctive leather helmets with red and black plumes. Lafayette's Corps, numbering approximately 2,000 men, was organized into two brigades of three battalions each. After the reduction in Continental forces after difficult winter quarters in February, 1781 Lafayette took command of a somewhat smaller brigade of 1,200 men in three battalions. Both the Light Corps, now fully established as a permanent independent unit, and Wayne served together in the 1781 Virginia campaign. Wayne, with the Pennsylvania division, joined Lafayette in the late spring and engaged in the preliminary maneuvering that ultimately led to Cornwallis'

---

1   Quoted in Johnson, *The Storming of Stony Point*, p.131.

surrender at Yorktown. Among those British surrendering at Yorktown was Lieutenant Colonel Henry Johnson.

Johnson spent several months in American captivity which allowed him time to reflect on the events of 15 July. He and other officers were exchanged in December, 1780. Johnson should not have been surprised that the subject of the loss of Stony Point was still being discussed among the British staff and Loyalists in New York. Recognizing that his reputation was at stake Johnson requested a court martial to clear his name. The proceedings began on 2 January 1781 with testimony from 22 officers and men, including Johnson. The Court examined the condition of the defenses, the adequacy of plans to respond to an attack, the utilization of the artillery, the size of garrison and the role of the support vessels in the Hudson River. After a month of testimony the Court returned a verdict on 20 February. Despite clear evidence that Johnson misunderstood the need to defend the Upper Works in lieu of the Lower Works, ignored recommendations to improve the defenses, and failed to ensure proper coordination to utilize the artillery to defend the fortifications the Court found Johnson guilty of only being 'culpable' for the errors, which the Court nevertheless found 'reprehensible'. Paradoxically the Court then concluded that Johnson, his officers and men 'behaved with an Alertness, Activity and Bravery, that do them Honor'. With his honor only slightly tarnished Johnson returned to the army, serving through the remainder of the American War and achieving the final rank of lieutenant general in 1799. It is interesting to note that Johnson's biography, written in the early 19th century, in summarizing his military service makes no mention of his role at Stony Point.[2]

---

2   John Philippart (ed.) *The Royal Military Calendar or Army Service and Commission Book*, (London: A.J. Valpy, 1820), Vol.I p.346

Appendix

Orders of Battle

Organization of the Continental Corps of Light Infantry
Brigadier General Anthony Wayne
Captain Henry Fishbourne, aide
Henry Archer, aide

1st Light Infantry Regiment
Colonel Richard Butler

> **1st Battalion** Major John Steward
> 4 Companies Maryland Light Infantry

> **2nd Battalion** Lieutenant Colonel Samuel Hay
> 4 Companies Pennsylvania Light Infantry

2nd Light Infantry Regiment
Colonel Christian Febiger

> **1st Battalion** Major Thomas Posey
> 4 Companies Virginia Light Infantry

> **2nd Battalion** Lieutenant Colonel Francois-Louis Fleury
> 4 Companies Virginia Light Infantry

3rd Light Infantry Regiment
Lieutenant Colonel Jonathan Meigs

> **1st Battalion** Lieutenant Colonel Isaac Sherman
> 4 Companies Connecticut Light Infantry

> **2nd Battalion** Lieutenant Colonel Henry Champion
> 4 Companies Connecticut Light Infantry

4th Light Infantry Regiment
Major William Hull

> **1st Battalion** Major William Hull
> 4 Companies Massachusetts Light Infantry
>
> **2nd Battalion** Major Hardy Murfee
> 2 Companies Massachusetts Light Infantry
> 2 Companies North Carolina Light Infantry

·≍≭≍·

British Garrison Stony Point, 15 July 1779
Commander Lieutenant Colonel Henry Johnson

> **17th Foot** Lieutenant Colonel Henry Johnson (380)
> **Grenadier Companies, 71st Highlanders** Captain L.C. Campbell (158)
> **Loyal American Company** Captain Morris Robinson (68)
> **Royal Artillery** (50)

·≍≭≍·

American Order of Battle, 15 July 1779

Right Attack Column: (933)
Forlorn Hope (20) Lieutenant George Knox
Advance Company (150) Lieutenant Colonel Francois-Louis Fleury
Main Column (763) Colonel Christian Febiger
        Lieutenant Colonel Jonathan Meigs
        Major William Hull

Left Attack Column: (455)
Forlorn Hope (20) Lieutenant James Gibbons
Advance Company (100) Major John Steward
Main Column (335) Colonel Richard Butler

Diversionary Detachment: (87)
Major Hardy Murfee

Bibliography

Anon. 'Founders Online', National Archives, last modified February 1, 2018, at
    http://founders.archives.gov

Barnes, James, *The Hero of Stony Point, Anthony Wayne* (New York: D. Appleton,
    1916).

Berg, Fred Anderson, *Encyclopedia of Continental Army Units* (Harrisberg:
    Stackpole, 1972).

Buell, Rowena, *The Memoirs of Rufus Putnam* (Boston: Houghton, Mifflin and
    Company, 1903).

Braisted, Todd W., *Grand Forage, 1778* (Westholme: Yardley, 2016).

Campbell, Maria, *Revolutionary Services and Civil Life of General William Hull*
    (New York: D. Appleton, 1848).

Canon, Richard, *Historical Record of the Seventeenth, The Leicestershire Regiment of
    Foot* (London: Parker, Furnivall and Parker, 1848).

Clarke, Samuel G. 'William Hull', *New England Historical and Genealogical Register*,
    47 (April-July 1893), pp.141-153.

Clinton, Henry (ed. William Willcox), *The American Rebellion: Sir Henry Clinton's
    Narrative of His Campaigns, 1775-1782, with an Appendix of Original
    Documents* (New Haven, Connecticut: Yale University Press, 1954).

Dawson, Henry, *The Assault on Stony Point by General Anthony Wayne, Gleanings
    from the Harvest of American History* (New York: Morrisania, 1863).

Ford, Worthington Chauncey, *et al* (eds.) *Journals of the Continental Congress,
    1774-1789* (Washington, D.C.: Government Printing Service, 1904-37), Vol.11,
    pp.538-39.

Futhey, J. Smith, 'The Massacre of Paoli', *The Pennsylvania Magazine of History and
    Biography*, Vol. 1, No. 3, 1877, p..285-319.

Garden, Alexander, *Anecdotes of the American Revolution* (Charleston S.C.: A.E.
    Miller, 1828).

Hall, James, *Memoir of Thomas Posey*, The Library of American Biography, Vol. IX.
    (Boston: Little and Brown, 1846).

Howe, William, *The Narrative of Lieut. Gen Sir William Howe in a committee of the
    House of Commons,* (London: H. Baldwin, 1780)

Johnson, Henry P., 'Christian Febiger, Colonel of the Virginia Line of the
    Continental Army', *The Magazine of American History*, Vol. VI (1881), pp. 188-
    203.

Johnson, Henry P. *The Storming of Stony Point on the Hudson* (New York: White
    and Company, 1900).

Loprieno, Don, *The Enterprise in Contemplation: The Midnight Assault of Stony
    Point* (Westminster, Maryland: Heritage Books, 2009).

Martin, James Kirby, *Ordinary Courage, The Revolutionary War Adventures of
    Joseph Plumb Martin* (New York: St James, 1993).

McGuire, Thomas J. *Battle of Paoli* (Mechanicsburg: Stackpole Books, 2000).

McGuire, Thomas J. *The Philadelphia Campaign Volume II Germantown and the
    Roads to Valley Forge* (Harrisberg: Stackpole, 2007).

McMichael, Scott R. 'Proverbs of the Light Infantry', *Military Review* 65 (September 1985), p.21-28.

McMichael, Scott R., *A Historical Perspective on Light Infantry. Research Survey*, No. 6, (U.S. Army Command and General Staff College, Command Studies Institute, 1987).

Moore, H. N. *Life and Services of Gen. Anthony Wayne* (Philadelphia: Leary, Getz, 1845).

Palmer, Dave Richard, *The River and the Rock* (New York: Greenwood Publishing, 1969).

Pennypacker, Samuel W., 'Anthony Wayne', *Pennsylvania Magazine of History and Biography*, Vol. XXXII, (1908), p.257-301.

Philippart, John, *The Royal Military Calendar or Army Service and Commission Book* (London: A.J. Valpy, 1820).

Rankin, Hugh, *The North Carolina Continentals* (Chapel Hill: University of North Carolina Press, 1971).

Johnson, Henry P, 'Return Jonathan Meigs, Colonel of the Connecticut Line of the Continental Army', *The Magazine of American History with Notes and Queries*, Vol. IV (1880), pp.281-292.

Sklarshy, I.W., *The Revolution's Boldest Venture* (Port Washington: Kennikat Press, 1965),

Spears, John R. *Anthony Wayne* (New York: D. Appleton, 1903).

Stille, Charles J. *Major General Anthony Wayne and the Pennsylvania Line in the Continental Army* (Philadelphia: Lippincot Company, 1893).

Townshend, Charles Hervey, *The British Invasion of New Haven, Connecticut, Together with Some Account of Their Landing and Burning of the Towns of Fairfield and Norwalk, July 1779*, (New Haven, Connecticut, 1879)

Wilcox, William B. *Portrait of a General* (New York: Knopf, 1962).

Wright, John W., 'The Corps of Light Infantry in the Continental Army', *The American Historical Review*, April 1926, Vol. 31, No. 3 pp.454-461.